My Stand

By: Julianne Benzel

Foreword by
Dennis Prager

-Classic Liberal, where are you? You were once heard espousing, "I Disapprove of What You Say, But I Will Defend to the Death Your Right to Say It." Please come back.

-The Best Teachers Show You Where to Look but Don't Tell You What to Think

Foreword by
Dennis Prager

One of the guiding principles of my career, the motto of my national radio show for 35 years, has been "I prefer clarity to agreement."

Julianne Benzel's story embodies this motto. You may not agree with this wonderful public school teacher, but her story makes clear where we are as a society, particularly the state of our public schools.

I first "met" Mrs. Benzel on March 19, 2018 when I interviewed her on my radio show. There was a national walkout scheduled the week prior in public schools across the country in the wake of the terrible shootings at Stoneman Douglas High School in Florida. The walkout was intended to express support for gun control laws.

This raised an important issue: Students do not lose their First Amendment rights to free speech simply because they are on a school campus, but should schools support students in what would otherwise have been considered truancy? Thousands of schools decided to offer such support, whether explicitly or implicitly.

Julianne Benzel's was among them. Everyone knew the walkout was in support of gun control, which is, of course, generally considered a liberal-leaning cause. Nevertheless, Mrs. Benzel, a lifelong conservative, fully supported the right, and indeed what she believes a duty, of her students to protest on behalf of the causes they believe in. As an AP US History teacher, she deeply believes in the right of every American to protest and have their government listen to their voices on the pressing issues of the day. That is, after all, one of America's bedrock principles. And Julianne Benzel wanted to ensure that her students also ascribed to this bedrock principle, or at least challenge them on whether they did or not.

So, several days before the walkout, Mrs. Benzel asked her students whether they would support the right of other students to protest during school hours if it was a conservative issue, such as a pro-life walkout? In other words, would they support the right of their fellow students to do the very same thing they did, if they disagreed with them?

This was, of course, an entirely reasonable question, one which Mrs. Benzel encouraged her students to consider and discuss. Moreover, she took no side because, the excellent teacher that she is, she was more interested in teaching students how to think, rather than what to think. She encouraged her students to consider, discuss, and debate the issue to arrive at a better, more informed conclusion. The conclusions they reached were up to them.

That, however, was unacceptable to her school district.

The morning of the walkout, Mrs. Benzel was notified that she had been put on paid administrative leave. She was given no explanation, despite the fact that she was a beloved and widely acclaimed teacher of 20 years at Rocklin High School.

Local media got wind of the story, and even learned the reasons for her suspension before Mrs. Benzel did. The story then went viral, with Mrs. Benzel appearing on national media such as Fox News and my radio show.

Some will agree and some will disagree with Mrs. Benzel's actions. Likewise, some will agree and some will disagree with her school district. But what is most important is the clarity this incident has brought. And it is clear that in our public schools, not all political ideas are equal. It is clear that in our public schools, some do not have the same right to protest as others. It is clear that in American public schools, there is an overwhelmingly left-leaning agenda at work. And it is clear that this agenda means indoctrinating students in left-wing ideas supersedes teaching them.

This was not an isolated incident. Stories like Mrs. Benzel's are the rule in most of America's public schools, (and most of the private ones as well.) If Americans do not come to realize this, America 's future as a free society, based on values that have guided this country since its founding, is in genuine jeopardy.

One point is worth emphasizing: Neither I, nor Mrs. Benzel, believes that one must be a Conservative to agree with the stand she takes in this book. In fact, you could be a passionate Liberal, completely agree with her, and disagree with the politicization of our public school system. In fact, Mrs. Benzel received many messages of support from just such Liberals who were disgusted by the Leftist manipulation of the school system that is supposed to serve all of us. Free speech, protest, and critical thinking are something we all can, and all should value—regardless of our political opinions. They are what makes America—America.

Julianne Benzel is the sort of teacher every American should want to teach their child. Not because she is a Conservative, but because she is more interested in her students learning how to think, not what to think. But the public school system she has served her entire adult life frequently prefers the opposite. It has too often put a one-sided political agenda ahead of truly educating our young people.

Free speech and critical thinking are just as much liberal values as they are conservative- but they are anathema to the Left, which apparently believes it cannot prevail through persuasion when dissenting views are tolerated. As Mrs. Benzel says at the end of her book: "There is room for disagreement, yes. But there is never room for blatant and overt silencing of any one or any idea. This is what we must continue to stand against."

This book is very important. It is a proverbial wake-up call. And it is written by someone who has the rarest of all human traits-courage.

Author's Note

This book is primarily about my years at Rocklin High School, of which I have nothing but fond memories interacting and engaging in a beautiful exchange of ideas with my students. I would therefore like to make something painstakingly clear: This is not meant to serve as an attack on my specific campus in any way. I am certain that my story is not necessarily unique in that conservative voices are routinely silenced in the education profession; I imagine this is happening all over the country and deserves the attention this book is giving it. I live in Placer County, which is one of the few remaining "red" spots in California; if this is happening in a mostly conservative region, I can only imagine how difficult it must be in other places throughout the state and country to be a conservative in certain professions.

Also, the need for a makeover in education is a much-needed conversation that can take place at another time. School and parental choice are imperative initiatives to address the educational crisis if we are going to be competitive as a country in the 21st century. I have a few specific classroom reform models that have peaked my interest, and I will be exploring those further as I continue in this new venture as a candidate.

That being said, Rocklin High School started out as a very unique and special place. Its founding principal was an innovating and "out of the box" thinker who pioneered the concept of Mastery Learning. Although controversial at the time, this model has been adopted not only by public schools nationwide but also by junior and community colleges.[1] The staff at Rocklin High School has always operated as a family; most of us living and raising our own kids within the same community. If there were disagreements or varying viewpoints, they were discussed and dealt with reasonably. As I refer to the several "stands" in this book that I have taken throughout my twenty years, the administrators previously in charge never intervened in these discussions; they allowed us as teachers to work through them as professionals because they trusted our ability to resolve them and they were not afraid of open and frank dialogue.

The staff at Rocklin High School works tremendously hard to serve the needs of students and parents; this has always been the case and it continues to be so today. But within the past few years some things have certainly changed, coinciding I believe, with the divisive climate of our country. There is a distinct new tone to the campus that operates in fear and control. A "fall in line," very "top down," bureaucratic management approach has been implemented that does not work well in the realm of education, where constant input is vital and necessary from the educators who are actually in the classroom with their students. It is in this atmosphere and under these dynamics that my ultimate stand and story unfolds. It must also be stated that everything in this book is completely, factually accurate; as breathtaking as some of this may seem, there has been no fabrication at all. I have also chosen not to reveal specific names as they relate to the events in each chapter, because it is not the individuals that matter but rather what has occurred in my twenty years that is key to the story here.

---

[1] http://www.ijonte.org/FileUpload/ks63207/File/chapter_8.pdf

Table of Contents

Preface

"They used our students as pawns to target you; they did not go down to the office voluntarily to complain about your discussion, but rather were called out of class by the female vice principal. They were each called down separately and no one else was in the room, like a parent or other adult should have been. They asked leading questions to attain the narrative that they desired and wanted. I know these things first hand because I conduct interviews for a living. Our students were really upset when they heard you were placed on leave and how this harmed you, and said they were confused and felt used."

-Rocklin High School Parent

"Wait, *what*!?" was my immediate response to what this parent had just told me. We were meeting together in the conference room at the Rocklin High School front office when I learned of this new and startling revelation. "What do you mean?" I asked. The statement that the school district gave to the media that "several students and parents complained about how this teacher communicated in class regarding the student-led remembrance activities is why she was placed on administrative leave" was *sought out*? Is that what you're saying? They went on a "hunting expedition" to get information? They manipulated my students to craft a complaint that wasn't even real? They manufactured fictitious evidence? This particular aspect of the story has never been told, but the conversation that ensued at this parent's initiation and request is perhaps far more frightening than anything that happened to me in the now infamous "teacher placed on administrative leave for questioning the National School Walkout" story.

My Stand was born the day I asked my American History students a few very simple questions: "Are you aware of the events scheduled to take place next Wednesday, March 14th? Are your parents aware? What are your thoughts...is it appropriate for our administration, or any administration throughout the country, to condone and facilitate a "gun protest walkout" during classroom instructional time? Do you think they would give the same courtesy to another group with a conservative bent, such as a Pro Life walkout?" For asking my students to be "free thinkers" by posing these basic, yet essential 1st amendment questions, I was placed on administrative leave by my school district at 8:30 am on the scheduled day of the National School Walkout. No reason or justification was given to me when I was placed on leave, nor was I told how and why that decision was made.

In actuality, my stand did not really *begin* at that moment, it was simply unveiled to the nation that day. My Stand chronicles the key moments when I challenged the subtle but powerful political persuasions that I encountered over the past twenty years as an American History instructor; documenting a long train of incidents, speaking truth to power. I have always been a fierce defender of "free speech and fair play." If one side of an argument is presented, then a counter argument must follow to arrive at an objective conclusion. All voices and sides of an issue should be heard, correct? But this is rarely the case in public and higher education today. We have seen throughout the annals of world history the horrors of what occurs when dissenting opinions are marginalized; and now our own American democratic Republic is at a serious crossroads: Are we going to adhere to our basic founding principles of due process and equal protection, or silence and punish those with whom we disagree? I therefore share in the following chapters a brief and concise narrative of the key moments when, with great conviction, I took a Stand - finding that I could not just sit idly by on the sidelines or follow the herd, a mentality that is far too common in society today. I hope that you too will find the courage and boldness to take your own Stand in whatever arena you find yourself, and whomever or whatever forces come up against you. This book will also lay out and help clarify how being placed on administrative leave led to my decision to file with the FEC to run for POTUS in 2020. It is my sincere desire that you hear my heart through the following pages: I am a historian, not a politician; my craft is to attain objectivity over hyperbole. This is who I am, this is my platform.

My Stand

I. Columbine

"[I]f men are to be precluded from offering their sentiments on a matter, which may involve the most serious and alarming consequences, that can invite the consideration of mankind, reason is of no use to us; the freedom of speech may be taken away, and, dumb and silent we may be led, like sheep, to the slaughter."

-George Washington to Officers of the Army, 1783

As I began to reflect on my 20 years of teaching, I started out as I imagine all educators do...with a beautiful sense of naïveté and optimism that I could truly change the world, one student at a time. In September, just one month into teaching, I met the love of my life. He was a co-teacher in our department and the head football coach. We fell in love and married six months later in April 1998. We, therefore, began our journey together, investing all of our time and energy into our students, and the Rocklin High School campus and community in general.

On April 20, 1999, the horrific and tragic events of the Columbine school shootings occurred. Eric Harris and Dylan Klebold, two very sinister and disturbed teenagers, originally sought to blow up their entire school; instead they went on a deadly rampage, killing 13 innocent victims before taking their own lives. My own personal sense of optimism was certainly shattered that day as the world watched in utter shock and dismay as the events unfolded. Two disgruntled students brought semi-automatic weapons to their high school campus and killed their classmates at random? How can this be? So many questions still linger and remain unanswered today, but one thing does not: school campuses were now "soft targets" for mass shooters... this thought alone was frightening and surreal. But so was another... as a result of Columbine, high School campuses also became "soft targets" for political activists with a very specific agenda, and Rocklin High School was certainly no exception.

In response to the mass school shooting, Left wing activist Michael Moore produced a documentary film in 2002 called *Bowling for Columbine*. The film explores what Moore suggests are the primary causes for the high school massacre in 1999 and other acts of violence with guns. Moore specifically targets and condemns the 2nd amendment and the National Rifle Association. It is his fundamental right as an American citizen to produce such a film and present it to the rest of the world, as indeed he did. A critical and commercial success, the film brought Moore international attention as a rising filmmaker and won numerous awards, including the Academy Award for Best Documentary Feature, the Independent Spirit Award for Best Documentary Feature, a special *55th*

Anniversary Prize at the 2002 Cannes Film Festival, and the César Award for Best Foreign Film.[2] However, does the success of the film mean we should expose and indoctrinate our young and malleable students with Moore's perceived vision of truth? The answer, of course, is no. But (unfortunately) that is not how some fellow teachers on my Rocklin High School campus felt. In the spring of 2003, during one of our department staff meetings it was suggested that,

> "Hey, I think we should all show Michael Moore's *Bowling for Columbine* documentary to our students."

I was initially taken aback because this was a World History teacher, so I did not see the connection to any of his curriculum, or any other curriculum in our department, except perhaps Government.

"Hold on a minute," I said, "why would we do that?" (Anything with Michael Moore attached to it must be met with extreme caution, as he has a one sided and very clear agenda in all of his work. So, this is where my first, albeit small, stand took place, yet it started a very clear trajectory for me on my high school campus.)

"Hold on? Why?" asked a colleague.

---

[2] https://www.documentary.org/magazine/michael-moores-bowling-columbine-2002

"Michael Moore?," I responded, "You want us to show his film to all of our students?"

"Sure!" they exclaimed.

I responded, "Why, again?"

No answer was provided.

So I asserted, "Um, no thank you."

Gasps throughout the room.

"Why not? What's wrong with that?" they questioned.

"*Bowling for Columbine*, shown in class?" I rebutted.

"If we show a Michael Moore documentary film to our students that casts all of the blame entirely on guns, then are we willing to broadcast a Rush Limbaugh radio show to discuss the 2nd amendment show the other side?"

The room was suddenly silent, tension thick. Those teachers who suggested we show the film looked at me and were literally aghast; one of them saying,

"You are joking, right? Please tell me you're joking? *Rush Limbaugh*, really? How could you even suggest such a thing?" To which I quipped, "No, I'm not joking. You want to show Michael Moore, so why not broadcast Rush Limbaugh also? Do you not see the double standard here?"

They unfortunately did not seem to realize that if we chose to expose our students to Michael Moore's perspective, then we must verse them in Rush Limbaugh's or another conservative viewpoint also, correct? Seemed fair enough to me! It was incredulous to me that Michael Moore was perceived as reasonable and fair, whereas the mere mention of the name Rush Limbaugh was high heresy. I immediately invoked the "academic freedom" clause in our teaching contract to firmly denounce this attempt at indoctrination; I made it clear that I would not be showing it to my students. Many in my department were less than pleased with me.

This stand was early on in my career and may seem silly or irrelevant to some, but the "peer pressure" to shut up, fall in line, and don't you dare bring up the "other side" was evident already. I was branded "controversial" and probably a few other choice words as well. One must also understand the backdrop of a high school community: There is an intentional and fierce campaign to create a culture of pride and unity on the campus, which is understandable and respectable, no doubt. My husband, being the head football coach, has always carried this heavy burden with him: "Friday Night Under the Lights," and the success that hopefully ensues, is seen as a major catalyst for the rest of the school years' spirit and enthusiasm for the "We Are Rocklin" mantra. For me to question anything or anyone is genuinely seen as an "annoyance" or "hindrance" to the continuity that most are striving to attain. It was not easy to interject on that day and "stop the flow" of what many thought was a great idea to show Michael Moore's film. It would have been easy and more convenient if I just kept my mouth shut. Agreed. But, as one of my favorite historians and prolific authors of the colonial era, Laurel Thatcher Ulrich, professes in her book, "Well behaved women seldom make history." [3]

Speaking truth to power is not easy. It's uncomfortable; often viewed as divisive. It can be desperately lonely too. I recall sitting in that staff meeting questioning whether to show Moore's film, looking around at what I thought were like-minded and fair colleagues; or at least ones who would challenge this blatant attempt at political indoctrination, but no one else spoke up... or even came to aid or abet my question. *Hmmm, really? Am I genuinely the only one who doesn't think this is a good idea?* Perhaps if we did show *Bowling for Columbine* and then presented a counter argument from a conservative viewpoint, it could have been a valuable exercise in critical thinking and analysis. As a social science department, we could have collaborated and created a lesson plan that took a hard look at the evidence and data and ask some provocative questions: What were the Founding Fathers' intention when they inserted the Second

---

[3] Ulrich, Laurel Thatcher. *Well Behaved Women Rarely Make History.* New York: Random House, 2007.

Amendment into the Bill of Rights? Is access to guns what caused Eric

Harris and Dylan Klebold to go on a killing spree at their high school?

Would limiting or outlawing guns have prevented such a tragedy? What

sensible laws and restrictions can we enact as a country to maintain the

safety and security of all Americans? These questions are not genius in any

way, but are an avenue to get students (and adults) to think analytically on

a very complex issue: gun control. Myopic conversations on a wide range

of issues today is what has stifled creative and thoughtful solutions, and

continues to do so.

Let's do a brief but worthy exercise to prove my point: Thomas

Jefferson, anti-Federalist and states rights' proponent extraordinaire,

himself clearly grappled with the meaning of owning and possessing

weapons. Jefferson wrote this into the 1776 draft of the Virginia

Constitution, the first such document of a state declaring their

independence: **"No free man shall ever be debarred the use of arms."**

Not much to debate, now is there? Wait just a minute. We must now

consider that the second and third drafts of the same document added

"within his own lands or tenements" to the sentence. Does that change

things? Perhaps. It appears that Jefferson considered that there might be

some limitations on the individual's right to gun ownership. He seems to

be grappling with the idea that it is sensible to own a gun for self-defense on your own property, but perhaps another set of issues comes up when this gun is taken into public space?[4] Yes, the complexity. We have to truly *think.* No clear and concrete answers here.

And, if we fast forward approximately 200 years, we can see that the debate and questions surrounding the Second Amendment and its proper role in society have only intensified. Those opposed to the Second Amendment, and who argue in favor of strict gun control laws, focus primarily on *how* a mass shooter gains access to a murderous weapon; they seek ways to prevent guns getting into the hands of the wrong person by enacting stringent laws to ensure a tragedy by gun violence never occurs again. Admirable indeed, right? I'm not sure there's a person out there who wouldn't enact any measures necessary to prevent another mass shooting, but are gun laws really the answer?

Let's switch to the opposing view, shall we? Dennis Prager carefully argues that, "Most Americans believe that it is their right — and even their duty — to own guns for self-protection. Unique among major democratic and industrialized nations, Americans have traditionally believed in relying on the state as little as possible."[5] Many of those in favor of the Second Amendment suggest the other side has it all wrong:

---

[4]https://www.monticello.org/site/jefferson/no-freeman-shall-be-debarred-use-arms-spurious-quotation

[5] http://www.dennisprager.com/the-right-does-have-answers-on-guns-mr-president

Rather than focusing on how the shooter got the gun, they seek to find *why* the shooter committed such heinous acts in the first place. The mental health and well-being of the shooter must be examined and seen as the real root of the crime. More focus and resources should be poured into ways of preventing a mass shooting rather than quickly jumping to gun control laws. As one gun rights activist asserts:

"If truth and common sense were applied to this issue then the general population would all be privy to the knowledge that less than 3% of gun crimes are committed with weapons legally purchased and stored by the assailant. They would also be made aware that loopholes in background checks and at gun shows, making the legal purchase of guns easier, do not exist. As someone who has gone through the process at both stores and gun shows I can tell you a federal background check, safety exams, permits and license fees, as well as filing out numerous government forms all had to be completed before I entered my 10-day waiting period to pick up my gun. The general population would and *should* know the firearm sales and manufacturing industry in the USA is highly regulated and highly scrutinized. Almost all, 96%-98%, of gun deaths caused with a legally purchased firearm are suicides and accidents."[6]

As a historian, an originalist to the Constitution, yet someone who has never owned a gun before, I must rely on the data and evidence (even

---

[6]http://time.com/longform/both-sides-gun-control/9

though they are often uncomfortable and inconvenient). Here's some evidence that just came out as a result of the Jewish Synagogue shooting in Pittsburgh, PA:

A recent study in *JAMA* found that the US leads the developed world in civilian gun violence. The study found that the US had a rate of 10.6 gun deaths per 100,000 people in 2016, compared to Switzerland's rate of 2.8, Canada's 2.1, Australia's 1, Germany's 0.9, the United Kingdom's 0.3, and Japan's 0.2.[7]

Pretty grim statistics, to be sure. The commonality in most mass shootings, from Sandy Hook to Orlando to the Las Vegas Massacre, is the AR 15 rifle was used. Developed in the 1950s for the military, a variant of it was first used in the Vietnam War.[8] The question ensues...should civilians own assault weapons? And yet, mass shootings account for only a tiny portion of all gun deaths; handguns are by far the weapon of choice.[9] So, yet again, we find ourselves with no easy answers. Complex issues deserve thoughtful and careful consideration; extreme talking points do nothing to solve the issue.

Perhaps a better suggestion on the part of my colleagues to verse our students in this highly charged issue would have been to read

---

[7] https://www.vox.com/policy-and-politics/2018/10/29/18035634/trump-pittsburgh-synagogue-mass-shootings-guns
[8] https://www.npr.org/2018/02/15/586172062/why-the-ar-15-is-americas-rifle
[9] https://www.bbc.com/news/world-us-canada-41488081

something along the lines of the November 5, 2018 *Time* Magazine article on *Guns in America*; a breathtaking and sweeping project that is embedded with hard facts and sincere analysis. A broad spectrum of people from all across America was asked how and why they hold their particular stance on guns.[10] One comes away from reading this project asking more questions than receiving answers, but that's o.k. It allows for deep and critical thinking to occur, which should be the ultimate goal of all teachers for their students. It also allows for some clarity and perhaps even understanding of why people view guns in America so differently. Having utter contempt for someone who does not think in the same manner that you do is exactly what I have argued against and resisted my entire teaching career.

I genuinely welcome dissenting opinions and insist they are vital for a thriving democracy. As three of my favorite iconic women in history put it:

"I've always felt that a person's intelligence is directly reflected by the number of conflicting points of view he can entertain simultaneously on the same topic."

-Abigail Adams

---

[10] https://www.magzter.com/preview/12427/310325

"If we grow contemptuous of our fellows and consciously limit our intercourse to certain kinds of people whom we have previously decided to respect, we not only tremendously circumscribe our range of life, but limit the scope of our ethics."

-Jane Addams

"It is not only important but mentally invigorating to discuss political matters with people whose opinions differ radically from one's own."

-Eleanor Roosevelt

I know this all too well because I grew up in a house with a liberal agnostic father and a conservative Christian mother. Christmas celebrations were lively, to say the least. Yet, they were healthy and essential to who I became. I am firm in my convictions, and more often than not, hearing opposing views actually reinforces what I believe. But again, therein lies the beauty of taking a stand. Rather than being led by the masses and presumed to be in agreement with those in power, we must be confident enough to question and challenge - even when it's difficult or uncomfortable.

And that is precisely what I intended to do when I asked m students about the National Gun Walkout Protest. Making a rationale, informed decision should be a top priority for all Americans. Survey after survey taken during and after the protest that day revealed that a majority of the students who got up and walked out of class on March 14, 2018 had no real idea why they were doing so.[11] The guise that the walkout was to honor the 17 victims of the Parkland, FL shooting was shameful and misleading.[12] It was an avenue for gun control activists to manipulate and push their prescribed agenda. An uneducated and ill-informed electorate (or in this case of high school students, the soon to be electorate) is the gravest threat to a real democracy. Politicians and pundits who exploit and manipulate a tragedy to further their own agenda are contemptible to say the least.

What purpose did the Gun Walkout Protest serve anyway? If we are looking for real solutions, they will not arise out of baseless accusations. Are gun control laws better left to individual states? This is a topic of continued interest. The 9th Circuit Court of Appeals just ruled in *Young v Hawaii* that, "Gun rights is one of the most hotly debated issues in U.S. political and legal circles with any loosening or restriction of access to

[11]http://www.latimes.com/opinion/readersreact/la-ol-le-gun-control-walkout-voters-20180315-story.html
[12] http://www.wctv.tv/content/news/Schools-address-walkout-476685843.html

guns often leading to a court battle. We do not take lightly the problem of gun violence," Judge Diarmuid O'Scannlain wrote in the ruling for the two-judge majority. "But, for better or for worse, the Second Amendment does protect a right to carry a firearm in public for self-defense."[13] It appears that Jefferson's grappling with this issue was fruitful after all.

Of one thing I am certain: this issue varies from region to region throughout the country. For example, a very dear friend of mine who grew up in Montana offered the following when we were discussing this: "Guns are not a problem in Montana. It's part of the culture and lifestyle; they're thrown in the back of a pickup truck and left there without another thought. If a fight breaks out at a bar, they handle it the old-fashioned way and brawl until there's a winner. No guns involved ever. When a person from Montana hears oversimplified talking points about gun control or repealing the 2nd amendment, they are naturally alarmed."

And then my friend from the Bay Area, who has never even touched a gun in her life, assured me: "It has never, ever crossed my mind to own a gun. It's not something I grew up with or around so I don't feel a personal need for it. I can understand why people in more suburban or rural areas might want them, though." I use these two simple examples to

---

[13] http://www.abajournal.com/news/article/9th_circuit_panel_finds_a_constitutional_right_to_openly_carry_agundistin9

illustrate that opinions vary greatly based on geography, and the complexity of this issue is real; long-term solutions are not going to come quickly.

However, school safety measures *must* be enacted; campuses can no longer be "soft targets." The world changed after 9/11 and our country took the necessary steps to ensure that another homeland attack would not occur. Why hasn't the same been done since Columbine? We must act *immediately* to protect our nation's most precious treasure: children. There are some basic changes that can and should be mandated for every single school in the country: additional police or armed guards on each campus, a primary or single point of entrance, and all classroom doors locked, period.

Let me provide you with a very real-life example of something that I experienced and the result could have been costly: It was our daughter's 7th birthday so I decided to surprise her and bring some Krispy Kreme doughnuts for her to share with the class mid-day. I had emailed her teacher the day prior to ensure this was permissible, and she agreed that it was. As I pulled into the circle in front of the school, the thought suddenly occurred to me that I could be *anyone* coming on to campus right now. It made me a little nervous, quite frankly, and so I purposely wanted to see what would happen if I went straight to the classroom without "checking in" with the front office. Answer: *nothing.* I got out of my car, in plain daylight, and walked right to my daughter's room, flung the door wide open with 3 dozen doughnuts, and said "surprise!" No one saw or stopped me along the way to ensure that I had checked in as a "visitor" and there was absolutely no impediment to my quick, easy and immediate access to my daughter's classroom. Instead of doughnuts in those boxes, I could have easily disguised murderous weapons. The notion that this could have ended in anything but happy was a thought that has haunted me ever since.

Do I blame my daughter's teacher? Not at all. She was gracious enough to answer my email request and allow me to bring the doughnuts in to share. Managing a classroom and fulfilling the obligation to cover the state's curriculum framework is a teacher's primary objective, but they have increasingly been asked to become mental health specialists, "mindfulness" coaches, and quasi-therapists whose job is now to be on the lookout for depressed, withdrawn, or excluded students. They should not have to take on the added burden of security experts as well.

Then who is to blame? The school board, superintendent, and site administrators. Although as a parent, I have received voluminous amounts of emails from the varying levels of administrators asserting that their "top priority is the safety of students," not *one* measure has been taken to ensure that. At the very least, with no cost to anyone, it should be mandated that classroom doors are locked from the inside; what would be prudent and a reasonable expense is to change the pads on every door to ensure that they automatically lock when closed, so as not to rely or put undue pressure on the teachers to remember to do so. This is a very minor, but potentially life-saving measure that has yet to be enacted in our local schools. I applaud other districts around the country who have taken preemptive measures to avoid a tragedy. Senator Ted Cruz from Texas just introduced logical legislation to get this trajectory in motion.[14] I fully support and applaud these efforts, which include:

(1) Controlling access to school premises or facilities, through the use of metal detectors or other measures, or technology, with evidence-based effectiveness...

(2) Implementing any technology or measure, or installing any infrastructure, to cover and conceal students within the school during crisis situations;

(3) Implementing technology to provide notification to relevant law enforcement and first responders during such a situation;

(4) Implementing any technology or measure, including hiring school security officers, or installing any infrastructure, with evidence-based effectiveness...to increase the safety of school students and staff;

(5) Implementing any technology or measure, or installing any infrastructure, for school safety reinforcement, including bullet-resistant doors and windows; and

---

[14]https://www.dailywire.com/news/34953/senator-ted-cruz-introduces-legislation-greatly-frank-camp

(6) Implementing any technology or system that would reduce the time needed to disseminate official information to parents regarding the safety of their children during and immediately following a crisis.

Aside from the horrific, and at the time extremely rare, tragedy at Columbine, mass school shootings were not the "norm" that they are today. An alarming, and almost unbelievable statistic is that 2018 has been deadlier for school children than military service members.[15] Something is gravely amiss in this country. Mass school shootings, or mass shootings of any kind, cannot continue to be the "new normal" in this country, they can and must stop; we will find a way.

---

[15] http://www.apa.org/pi/lgbt/resources/history.aspx

II. Minority Ruling the Majority

"The tyranny of the minority is infinitely more odious and intolerable and more to be feared than that of the majority."

-President William McKinley to the House of Representatives, 1886

Let me be very clear from the start: I grew up in Concord, California, officially part of the San Francisco Bay Area. I have friends from high school who are in same sex marriages with kids, who live just like the rest of us do; working hard at their jobs throughout the week, hitting the dirt at ball games on Saturdays, and enjoying lazy BBQs on Sundays. Whenever we get together to catch up, our time together is the same as it is with any other acquaintance.

Our next-door neighbor living in Rocklin was a lesbian woman (she has since passed away) whom we had over to our house several times and with whom we developed a real and lasting friendship. Some of the students I have been closest to have been gay or lesbian. I, personally, do not understand, nor am I genuinely comfortable with the homosexual lifestyle; I have poured over scripture after scripture and I do not find where this is God's will or plan for the human race. However, I am not anyone's judge, nor do I presume to know everything. What I am assured of is that if I view every single person in the same manner that Christ sees me, then I can never, ever go wrong.

I am not, nor will I ever be, interested in taking anyone's rights away. It absolutely must be acknowledged that the LGBTQ movement has been one of the most efficient, well organized, and massively funded movements in our nation's history.[16] The movement's ultimate victory came when the supreme court ruled in *Obergefell vs. Hodges* in 2015 by a 5-4 split that same-sex marriage was legal in all 50 states,[17] a decision made with such rapidity that one barely had time to digest its full extent. But the fact remains that same-sex marriage is the law of the land and it will not be overturned. Let me, once again, be very clear: I vehemently disagree with the *manner* in which the court ruled; this was judicial activism in its gravest form, and it is not the supreme court's job to legislate from the bench (refer to Article 1, section 1 and Article 3, section 1 of the U.S. Constitution if you need further clarification). It should have been up to each individual state to determine their own marriage laws, so this is an overreach by the bench that I neither appreciate nor condone. I do, however, understand the court's *rationale*. Invoking the due process clause and the 14th amendment's "equal protection under the law" is

---

[16] http://prospect.org/article/how-gay-rights-movement-won
[17] https://www.nationalreview.com/2015/06/gay-marriage-ruling-completes-secularization-of-america

indisputable. Same sex couples now have the constitutional right to marry and that will not be taken away. The next step now is to ensure that people like me, who are not hateful "homophobic bigots" as some would like to presume, but are genuine in their deep religious convictions regarding homosexuality, are afforded the same "due process and equal protection" of the law, and are not forced to agree or comply with the homosexual lifestyle, or be punished for our disagreeing. As Americans, we must, once again, reach a place of commonality and mutual respect regarding our differences.

What I *do* object to is the indoctrination of students, by anyone at any time. One thing is certain (and I have twenty years of first-hand experience to support this claim): High school, junior high, and elementary school kids are confused enough as to who they really are, and they have enough peer pressure coming at them from all directions. To add another dimension to who they may or may not become has no place at all on a public school campus. There is concrete biological evidence that the brain does not fully develop until 22-25 years of age,[18] so to make any long term, impactful decisions before this time is erroneous, at best. And public schools should not be a place of personal political persuasions.

---

[18] https://www.ncbi.nlm.nih.gov/pmc/articles/PMC3621648/

In 1996, the GSA and LGBTQIA (more acronyms have been added since they were first established) had formed clubs on high school campuses throughout the nation. They organized a "Day of Silence"[19] where students were encouraged to take a day-long vow of not talking to symbolically represent the discrimination and bullying of gay, lesbian, or transgender students. Due to first amendment rights, and the supreme court's ruling in *Tinker vs. Des Moines* in 1969[20], any and all clubs were valid and students could not be punished for protesting at school, *so long as it does not disrupt the instructional classroom time.* Hmmm, could get a little murky, right? Who gets to decide what is "disrupting school work?" School districts, site administrators, individual teachers? The ruling was terribly unclear here.

On the Rocklin High School campus, in the year 2005, the GSA/LGBT club advisor, who was a fellow teacher, sent out an all staff email stipulating that there would be a "Day of Silence" the following week. Teachers were encouraged to participate or "join in" to support the students by wearing T-shirts, buttons and other propaganda. The students were going to "remain silent all during the school day" as a way to bring awareness of the discrimination and bullying toward LGBTQ students.

[19]https://gsanetwork.org/resources/gsa-actions-events/day-silence

[20] https://constitutioncenter.org/blog/tinker-v-des-moines-protecting-student-free

Hmmm, I once again thought. *Really? Is this a good idea?* Lots of students are "bullied" for various reasons...why draw specific attention to this particular group and not "bullying" as a whole? Would this be allowed for any other group from the other, conservative side? I replied to the all staff email that, "Unless we as a staff are willing to endorse a Day of Silence for the millions of babies that are aborted every year who are *literally* silenced (not figuratively like the LGBTQ students) and will *never* have a voice, then I vehemently oppose, and will be requiring students to participate in classroom activities as if it were a normal day."

Oh, the backlash that ensued. I was quickly dubbed the "bigot teacher" and a "homophobic," (labels make everything quick and easy, don't they?) and of course, "how dare I"?!? "How could you oppose such a day? You're an educator...where is your tolerance?" Those who espouse "tolerance" only do so if you are in complete alignment with how *they* think. And let me make it extremely clear that I would be the absolute *first* person to defend any student who is being bullied, whether gay or straight. That is not the issue here.

When the "Day of Silence" came on the Rocklin High School campus, I specifically recall being shocked at other teachers wearing black T-shirts with bold white writing that said "Silent" and buttons with the same inscription. I'm quite confident that if I tried to rally students and teachers to protest for a conservative cause, it would not have been welcome in any way. And now teachers were being pitted against teachers and students against students. Can you just imagine if I had worn a T-shirt that day propagandizing the pro-life movement? Or what ridicule and scorn students who chose to be silent for the unborn that day would have faced? But of course, we will never know because no one dare ever bring up a conservative concept to protest...it was *unheard* of and not "politically correct."

One may stop and wonder...what's the big deal? Such hyperbole. Calm down, will you? What teacher wouldn't support the Day of Silence and want a chunk of their students to remain quiet and not talk for an entire day? I should have welcomed the relief, right? Hardly. The Day of Silence was not as disruptive as other protests could have been, but it was highly *inconvenient*. Teachers who planned a Socratic seminar or debate in class that day had to be sure not to call on the students who had tape over their mouths and the word "Silent" written across. What if presentations or speeches were due that day, then what? It was awkward to even have a normal discussion in my AP American History course because I usually call on students at random. The point is that students who remained silent that day were indeed accommodated, encouraged, and even applauded. And they continue to be accommodated; the Day of Silence occurs <u>every</u>

year in mid-April on public school campuses across the nation. No other group of students have a prescribed day every year to protest. The looming question remained...would the same teachers who validated this protest be so kind and courteous to another protest if it was conservative in nature? I think we already know the answer to that question. Not once in my two-decade teaching career has a conservative concept ever been brought up in an all staff email...*ever*. And when I had the gall to do so, I was placed on administrative leave.

There is no doubt that minorities need protection, irrelevant of the cause. The brilliance of the anti-Federalists' insistence that a Bill of Rights be added to the United States Constitution is to ensure that the majority alone does not rule. But tyranny of the mob cannot rule supreme either. A mere 3.8% of the American public identify themselves as gay or lesbian,[21] and barely on the radar at .6% are Americans who identify themselves as transgender.[22] Both of these groups need, and are guaranteed, equal protection under the law, but they consume a disproportionate amount of oxygen in the room in comparison to their numbers. When school locker rooms and bathrooms all over this country are being restructured to cater to a limited number of students, one must ask, are the rights of the majority being eclipsed at the expense of a very small minority? And more

[21] https://www.nytimes.com/2016/07/01/health/transgender-population.html
[22]https://www.cbsnews.com/news/transgender-reveal-kindergarten-class-rocklin-academy-parents-upset

importantly, are public schools (even down to the elementary level) the appropriate place for experimentations of this sort?

Case in point: In June 2017, a male kindergarten student in a Rocklin Academy Charter School asked his teacher to read a book titled "I Am Jazz" to the class. Co-written by biologically male teen Jazz Jennings, the book describes how Jazz "transitioned" from a boy to a girl. After the teacher read the book to the class, the male kindergarten student went to the bathroom and changed from his "boy clothes" into his "girl clothes." The teacher then instructed students to use the boy's new "girl name."[23] This is real, it actually happened. A classroom of five and six year olds were read a story about a how a boy turned into a girl and then one of their own classmates changed in the bathroom and insisted that he now be called "she" with a new name. Sigh. And the worst part of all? Parents of the kindergarten children were not asked or informed prior to this "coming out party." This is indoctrination at its deepest and most targeted level...children.

Does a five-year old really have any concept if he/she wants to change genders? Is it really appropriate for a teacher and school to support such an "unveiling" to other unsuspecting five- and six-year olds, without parent notification or consent? Many of the children were genuinely

[23]https://www.lifesitenews.com/news/mom-breaks-down-describing-effects-of-kindergarten-transgender-lesson

confused and upset by what they were forced to witness.[24] There is fierce psychological and medical research that concludes altering one's anatomy or hormones at an early age is extremely dangerous. Especially when we come to find out that, "70 to 80 percent of children with transgender feelings who received no medical or surgical treatment spontaneously *lost* those feelings. And given that close to 80% of such children would abandon their confusion and grow naturally into adult life if untreated, these medical interventions come close to child abuse." [25]

At the *bare minimum*, parents should be notified prior and have the right to opt out of LGBTQ curriculum that they are not comfortable with, especially at the elementary and junior high school levels. A very recent example in Colorado is when a self-described "drag queen" spoke to four classes of 6th-8th graders on "career day."[26] It was alarming for many of the kids, and their parents, to see a man dressed as a woman purporting the transgender lifestyle.

There *are* alternative viewpoints out there regarding the LGBTQ lifestyle but they are never recognized as valid or worthy of discussion. And those who hold them are marginalized at best. The Founding Fathers

---

[24] http://breakpoint.org/2017/06/breakpoint-opposing-the-transgender-craze/
[25] https://www.wsj.com/articles/the-transgender-battle-line-childhood-1451952794
[26] https://www.dailywire.com/news/37525/drag-queen-jessica-lwhor-visits-middle-school-james-barrett?fbclid=IwAR1185R-9wobEIFFJnmlxSpsgClfuGhfhVgiZMo2-mSM5szWUIODhOXJyFM

spoke at great length over the dangers of the "tyranny of the majority" when James Madison wrote in Federalist #10:

"By a faction, I understand a number of citizens, whether amounting to a majority or a minority of the whole, who are united and actuated by some common impulse of passion, or of interest, adverse to the rights of other citizens, or to the permanent and aggregate interests of the community. There are two methods of curing the mischiefs of faction: the one, by removing its causes; the other, by controlling its effects." [27]

And in Federalist #51:

"In a free government, the security for civil rights must be the same as that for religious rights. It consists in the one case in the multiplicity of interests, and in the other in the multiplicity of sects. The degree of security in both cases will depend on the number of interests and sects; and this may be presumed to depend on the extent of country and number of people comprehended under the same government."[28]

Alexis de Tocqueville took it one step further when he made his nine-month journey around the United States and penned his observations of *Democracy in America*:

---

[27]http://www.billofrightsinstitute.org/founding-documents/primary-source-documents/the-federalist-papers-10
[28] https://www.billofrightsinstitute.org/founding-documents/primary-source-documents/the-federalist-papers-51

"If it be admitted that a man possessing absolute power may misuse that power by wronging his adversaries, why should not a majority be liable to the same reproach? Men do not change their characters by uniting with one another; nor does their patience in the presence of obstacles increase with their strength. For my own part, I cannot believe it; the power to do everything which I should refuse to one of my equals, I will never grant to any number of them."[29]

It is imperative that the majority does not rule the minority but isn't the opposite true as well? Wouldn't it be just as erroneous if the minority is ruling the majority? Can you imagine the mayhem that would ensue if these varying viewpoints were dared to be mentioned in a classroom? Over the years, I personally have had several LGBTQ students and have treated them unequivocally the same as any other student. I've had a transgender student who is a girl insist she be called a certain name because she was now a boy. Everything that I saw from the outside was a girl...all of her features and her sweet, very feminine voice. I called her/him by her/his boy name but

---

[29] Alexis de Tocqueville, "Tyranny of the Majority," Chapter XV, Book 1, *Democracy in America*

what I would genuinely like to track is her/his life and see if she/he ends up being a "boy" after high school or college.

And when do you *ever* hear in the media of someone who has "changed back" from the homosexual[30] or transgender lifestyle?[31] As recently reported, "One of the world's top genital reconstructive surgeons says "sex change regret" is on the rise, and that more patients are coming to him to have their "gender confirmation" surgeries reversed — but that people, too afraid to be politically incorrect, just aren't talking about it.[32] Why isn't the LGBTQ community equally supportive of a boy who changed to a girl but then wants to go back to being a boy?[33] Yet the intentionality to get into the public school system has been this group's target from the beginning. School curriculum and textbooks have specifically been adopted in the state of California and are set to do so in other states, to highlight, celebrate and promote the LGBTQ movement.[34] In California, the Teacher's Union offers a $2,500 scholarship to anyone who identifies as gay, lesbian or transgender in hopes they will get into the education profession: The website reads: "*The **scholarship program** will*

---

[30]https://www.dailywire.com/news/30471/watch-ex-transgender-womans-powerful-testimony-im-amanda
[31]https://www.josephnicolosi.com/collection/celebrities-who-have-left-a-gay-lifestyle
[32]https://www.dailywire.com/news/37496/new-taboo-surgeon-says-sex-change-regret-rise-%E2%80%93-no-emily-zanotti
[33]https://www.thedailybeast.com/california-leads-the-way-teaching-lgbt-history-to-schoolchildren
[34] https://www.cta.org/en/About-CTA/CTA-Foundation/2016-Scholarships.aspx

*support **self-identified** LGBTQ members enrolled in a teacher/counseling credential or graduate program who are pursuing a career in public education and who understand the importance of LGBTQ educators as role models in our public schools.*"[35] Hmmm, I once again must ask...why are union dues being spent on recruiting one specific group of people into the teaching profession? Where is the scholarship for a conservative Christian teacher? I was never offered one of those. Or a Mormon, Muslim, Jew, Atheist, African American, Hispanic, Asian? Oh wait, that's right, those don't exist. The double standard is *everywhere.*

---

[35] https://www.cta.org/en/About-CTA/CTA-Foundation/2016-Scholarships.aspx

III. One President over the Other?

"Freedom is the right to tell people what they do not want to hear."

-George Orwell

There have been some pretty remarkable presidential speeches in my lifetime alone. I came of age, politically, in the 1980s at the height of the Reagan Revolution. Perhaps the peak came for me when I was just a freshman in high school on January 28, 1986:   the Space Shuttle *Challenger* exploded 73 seconds after takeoff, killing all 7 passengers on board, including a school teacher, Christa McAuliffe, who left behind her husband and two young children.[36] Oh the heartbreak. The newsreels were playing on every screen in America over and over, leaving us all wondering...how did this happen? The sense of optimism we had as Americans when the *Challenger* took off were dashed in despair mere moments later. We were looking for answers and we were looking for leadership.

President Reagan's speech following the *Challenger* explosion was nothing short of genius. And that is saying quite a lot knowing that two

[36] https://www.npr.org/sections/thetwo-way/2016/01/28/464744781/30-years-after-disaster-challenger-engineer

years earlier he gave his now infamous "Tear Down This Wall!" speech in Berlin, calling out Mikhail Gorbachev, which marked the beginning of the end of the decades long Cold War. [37] Reagan was scheduled to give the State of the Union address the night of January 28 but with the tragic events that unfolded that day, the SOTU speech would have to wait. And wait it did, because what followed when Reagan spoke to the nation that night was etched into the national conscience forever. As a fourteen-year old girl, I remember it like it was yesterday. "The crew of the space shuttle Challenger honored us by the manner in which they lived their lives," Reagan said. "We will never forget them, nor the last time we saw them, this morning, as they prepared for their journey and waved goodbye and 'slipped the surly bonds of earth' to 'touch the face of God.'"[38] Oh how those words resonated; they were powerful and potent; so beautifully woven into his speech and spoken perfectly by our beloved President.

I did not hear that speech at school, however. I do not recall any of my teachers ever mentioning or suggesting it. I watched the speech in the confines of my own home with my parents, whom I enjoyed a healthy dialogue and exchange with afterward. I have never watched or listened to a live presidential speech within the four walls of a classroom. It may or may not be appropriate to do so, and we can discuss and debate that at

[37] https://www.archives.gov/publications/prologue/2007/summer/berlin.html
[38] https://www.nytimes.com/2008/11/05/us/politics

another time; all I know is that in my experience as a student and a teacher, it had never occurred and was never suggested. That is, until the election of Barack Obama.

The world watched in sheer amazement as the United States elected its first Black president. [39] The pride and exuberance of that moment cannot be overstated. Racial barriers were going to fall and the world was just as it should be. A time for "hope and change" was in the air, and Americans were feeling reasonably united and proud as a country. All fair and good. But then came that September in 2009, just nine months after Obama was in office. He was set to give a "National Address to Schoolchildren," which was basically a "pep talk" on making the most of your educational opportunities.[40] Probably pretty harmless indeed. Except by this time into his presidency, Obama had already proven to be far more liberal than some Americans anticipated and the enthusiasm that ushered him into office was dissipating.[41] Perhaps the greatest benchmark of this early push back was his $789 billion spending stimulus package known as the American Recovery and Reinvestment Act,[42] passed in Congress a

---

[39] https://www.theguardian.com/world/2008/nov/05/barackobama-uselections2008
[40] https://obamawhitehouse.archives.gov/back-to-school
https://www.telegraph.co.uk/news/worldnews/barackobama/7030526/Barack-[41]Obama-review-of-pledges-kept-and-promises-broken-in-first-year.html
[41] https://www.npr.org/sections/itsallpolitics/2013/12/17/251983136/the-year-of-disappointing-the-liberal-base-obama-2013
[42] https://www.usnews.com/news/stimulus/articles/2009/02/12/summary-of-the-spending-programs-in-the-789-billion-stimulus-compromise

mere one month after he was inaugurated. Many Americans were not pleased with him adding almost $1 trillion to the already looming national debt.

Obama's "Back to School" speech was set for September 8, and arguably the most liberal teacher on the Rocklin High School campus, (with whom I interacted with more than anyone else because we genuinely enjoyed discussing politics, and we could do so amiably and respectfully; he is a *classic* liberal) sent out an all staff email suggesting that we, "all show Obama's speech to students in class because this is a historical moment and I think we should all be a part of it." Oh boy, I thought, here we go again... Historic time? Yes, it is, there is no doubt. But I am the history teacher here, and this thought never even crossed my mind. Why? Because I've never seen a live Presidential speech in a classroom environment; perhaps this was an improper mix of politics and education, I wondered? I was not alone. Backlash ensued throughout the country as many commentators suggested that this was an attempt at "blatant indoctrination of students to liberal ideas," and many parents wanted to see the text of the speech before their children were exposed.[43]

My response to the teacher's request over email was as follows: "I love and respect you very much, and you know that, but I am unsure if this

---

[43] https://www.politico.com/story/2009/09/school-speech-backlash-builds

is a wise decision. I appreciate and recognize the historical times we are living in but does that really mean we should all show Obama's live speech to our classes? Should it be shown even in the math, science and physical education classes? I do not recall ever being asked to show a live speech given by President George Bush, even after the events of 9/11, when one could make a concrete argument to do so. I do not think this is an appropriate venue to show Obama's speech," I concluded. The backlash from other teachers? You guessed it...not only was I a "bigot" but now I was also a "racist." Yup, a racist. That's me. Two teachers within my own social science department thought this was a "serious issue" and that it should be addressed. It (being me) "is a big problem here," they quipped. The brief dialogue over email continued and teachers were yet again pitted against teachers, with some chiming in, "I will happily show Obama's live speech to my class," while a few, rare others wondered what would happen if a student or parent had issue with this?

The school district sent out an "official statement" stipulating that teachers (and this funneled all the way down to the junior high and elementary levels) had the "option" of showing Obama's live speech in class, but they must allow students to "opt out" if they so choose. So, the day came and the speech was given and some teachers opted to show it, while others did not. Most students chose to remain in their class and watch it, while a few got up and walked out. Where did they go? Most teachers had no idea. And they were also unsure of when or if they would return to class. One student recalled, "I didn't care for Obama or his policies, and I had never been shown a live presidential speech in any class before, so when my Language Arts teacher said she was going to show it, I got up and walked out of class. She didn't know that I went to the library and stayed there for the rest of the period. I didn't know how long the speech was and she gave me no directive."[44]

Again, I beg the question... why are *some* ideas encouraged and condoned on public school campuses, and not others? Is this really what Horace Mann envisioned when he started to advocate for free public schooling in the 1840s? [45] I don't think so. Traditionally, Americans viewed education as a "three-way joint enterprise, involving the family, the church, and the school." Prior to this time, the school had been viewed as the least important part of this triad. In the eyes of those who opposed the public school movement, the school was now usurping the authority of the family and the church in order to proclaim itself as the foremost member of that triad. Interesting to note, that even in the 1840s it was readily apparent that a state supported school system was a wide open avenue of influence.

[44] Tanner DiBella, Student Oral Account of September 8, 2009
[45] http://www.theedadvocate.org/horace-mann-an-education-pioneer

When racial tensions started to flare up substantially during Obama's presidency, ignited by his comments suggesting that the Cambridge, MA police department "acted stupidly" when they arrested a college professor,[46] I thought for sure there would be some discussion on our high school campus regarding the issue of the African American community and its relationship with the police. But nothing at all was said. Then, after the Trayvon Martin shooting in Sanford, Florida, Obama interjected again stating that, "If I had a son, he would have looked like Trayvon." And he went on to suggest that there was a real crisis in America regarding race relations under the pretext and context of what it feels like to be a black man in America.[47]   The Black Lives Matter Movement quickly established itself as a political force as a result of the Trayvon Martin case with their professed statement of purpose: *Black Lives Matter is an ideological and political intervention in a world where Black lives are systematically and intentionally targeted for demise. It is an affirmation of Black folks' humanity, our contributions to this society, and our resilience in the face of deadly oppression.*[48]

[46]http://www.cnn.com/2009/US/07/22/harvard.gates.interview/
[47] https://obamawhitehouse.archives.gov/the-press-office/2013/07/19/remarks-president-trayvon-martin

[48] https://blacklivesmatter.com/about/herstory/

Because African Americans constitute approximately 20% of the United States population, I presumed that as a school staff we might actually *want and need* to discuss this issue; it certainly seemed worthy to at least suggest it? And then when the shooting of Michael Brown happened in Ferguson, Missouri in August of 2014, this had undoubtedly become a national issue and perhaps we should seize on a "teachable moment," at least within our own social science department. But not a word was spoken on these matters. The stories continued to pour in from community after community, the most recent here just 30 miles from my home in Sacramento, CA where Stephon Clark was shot 20 times by police in his grandmother's backyard.[49]

I have a very dear friend who is a 38-year old African American man, a respectable husband, father and member of his community who shared with me that since the age of 16 when he obtained his driver's license, he has been pulled over by the police 44 times. "Really?" was my initial response. "We are out here in so-called progressive, liberal California and this is happening? That seems excessive to me," I offered back. He further stated that his mom had "taught him right; to always respect officers and adhere to what they were asking me to do, so I immediately put my hands up every time I was pulled over so they knew I

[49] https://www.cnn.com/2018/03/22/us/sacramento-police-shooting/index.html

was not armed and I addressed them as sir or ma'am. Police officers have often said to me that I represent our 'kind' well." That brief but memorable conversation made me realize that these issues are real for African Americans in this country and particularly among Black men.[50] To suggest otherwise, or dismiss them altogether, is gravely unwise. Black lives *do* matter, as do *all* lives.

I revere and have the utmost respect for any man or woman in uniform; our police force put their lives in danger for the greater good every time they put their badge on. They are the unsung heroes in most cases, and yet their profession has been under assault by a media and fringe group who, in the extreme case, is calling for "dead cops."[51] I was startled, to say the least, when I saw policemen standing and protecting protesters who were, in turn, inciting violence with their rhetoric.[52] Of course, in America you can walk down the street with signs and chants calling for violence against the police who are standing there to ensure you have the right to say such a thing.

Toward the end of Obama's presidency in 2015, the Pew Research Center conducted a poll that found 58% of Americans saw racism as a "big problem" compared to 2011 when only 28% did.[53] Perhaps Obama's

---

[50] https://www.thedailybeast.com/the-monsters-who-screamed-for-dead-cops

[51] https://www.youtube.com/watch?v=dj4ARsxrZh8

[52]http://www.pewresearch.org/fact-tank/2017/08/29/views-of-racism-as-a-major-problem-increase-sharply

[53] http://jewishjournal.com/opinion/163840

interjection into the cases discussed above was not such a good idea after all, or perhaps he wasn't the President to unite the races, as most had hoped. There has been, without question, monumental gains achieved in race relations within the past 50 years; the Civil Rights Movement thrust this nation far beyond where it had lagged for decades. Three statistics that especially stand out are:

-In 1940, 60 percent of employed black women worked as domestic servants; today the number is down to 2.2 percent, while 60 percent hold white-collar jobs.

-In 1958, 44 percent of whites said they would move if a black family became their next-door neighbor; today the figure is 1 percent.

-In 1964, the year the Civil Rights Act was passed, only 18 percent of whites claimed to have a friend who was black; today 86 percent say they do, while 87 percent of blacks assert they have white friends.[54]

Positive progress is not usually reported in the mainstream media because it contradicts the narrative they are trying to push. The historic

---

[54] [54]https://www.brookings.edu/articles/black-progress-how-far-weve-come-and-how-far-we-have-to-go

election of our first Black President was indeed a milestone with much to celebrate, and remember it we shall. But it also revealed that we still have plenty of room for growth, and the discussion on race relations must continue in a respectful and meaningful way, whether on or off school campuses. There are plenty of ways to take a stand on behalf of the African American community without viewing or treating them as victims. And whether you agree with the Black Lives Matter movement or not, you have to at least respect the fact that their protesting takes place in the proper arena and they have not tried to do so within the four walls of a classroom.

IV. Cell Phones in Class...No!

"A people without the knowledge of their past history, origin and culture is like a tree without roots."

-Marcus Garvey

If it doesn't appear that I have already, I'm going to get a little "passionate," especially about this one...cell phones. For the vast majority of my teaching career, students have been engaged and mentally present for discussions, debates, and the everyday routines of a high school classroom. Great dialogue has taken place and students have been genuinely connected to each other. When the iPhone was introduced in 2007, we knew a revolution of sorts was about to occur - the world in our pocket, just a click or touch away.[55] Steve Jobs was a genius and we all had to get one. I've personally always been a little slow to catch on with technology and I don't apologize for it. I like traditionalism because some things simply never change. When my sister first encouraged me to send a text message, I quipped, "but I like conversing over the phone to people." She rolled her eyes and said in return, "just wait until you send one, you'll

[55]https://www.t3.com/features/a-brief-history-of-the-iphone

never be the same." And when I did send my first text, I knew immediately what she meant. Wow, that was fast, efficient, and I didn't have to speak a word...brilliant? Perhaps.

There's no returning from the cell phone craze, and I am not suggesting we throw them all away. Cell phones are a remarkable tool that enhance our lives, there's no question about that. But there *must* be limits. Study after study reveals that incessant time in front of any screen is harmful in a myriad of ways: not only to the brain itself, but our vision, sleep patterns, weight, attention capabilities, self-confidence, social skills, and overall mental health are affected.[56]

"Just trying to keep our own media and electronic files organized can be overwhelming. Each of us has the equivalent of over half a million books stored on our computers, not to mention all the information stored in our cell phones or in the magnetic stripe on the back of our credit cards. We have created a world with 300 exabytes (300,000,000,000,000,000,000 pieces) of human-made information. If each of those pieces of information were written on a 3 x 5 index card and then spread out side by side, just one person's share -- your share of this information -- would cover every square inch of Massachusetts and Connecticut combined. Our brains do have the ability to process the information we take in, *but at a cost*: We can have trouble separating the trivial from the important, and all this information processing makes us tired. Neurons are living cells with a metabolism; they need oxygen and glucose to survive and when they've been working hard, we experience fatigue. Every status update you read on Facebook, every tweet or text message you get from a friend, is competing for resources in your brain with important things like whether to put your savings in stocks or bonds, where you left your passport, or how best to reconcile with a close friend you just had an argument with."[57]

---

[56]https://smallbiztrends.com/2013/05/the-complete-history-of-social-media-infographic.html

[57] https://www.rallyhealth.com/health/unexpected-effects-screen-time

And, therefore, when a screen is readily available to you at any moment in your purse or pocket, it requires an incredible amount of discipline to be engaged and present with those around you. Disciplined habits are usually quite rare for adolescents and teenagers, so to allow unchecked and free range of cell phone use is foolish and extremely irresponsible.

But, once again, not everyone on my high school campus shared these viewpoints and they thought it was a "brilliant idea" to allow students to use their cell phones in class... "Let's get WiFi on campus and start using cell phones in class," one teacher suggested... "Think of the options! There's so many things they could do!" they quipped. Oh boy, I murmured to myself, this is the worst possible idea; we are opening a Pandora's box that will be *impossible* to close. I once again took a "stand" and made sure that at least my voice was heard, although I knew what the reaction to my resistance was going to be. I suggested, "Should we really be doing this? I'm not so sure. What about the possibility of students cheating on a test? Or taking pictures of a test? Or taking pictures in general, perhaps of other students without their permission?" My list of questions was actually endless, but a rebuttal was met with each one of them: "You can confiscate phones on test day. How would students take a picture of a test if they didn't have their phones? What would they want to take pictures of?" And on and on it went.

We do not give students enough credit for being the clever geniuses that they are...they find ways around "rules" that adults never even consider. For example, if a teacher decides to confiscate cell phones on exam day, then students bring a fake, "burner" one to turn in and then keep their actual cell phone in their pocket or backpack. When the teacher looks away, out comes the phone and in no time flat, they are discreetly on their device, looking up the answers. It's a brutal and endless cycle that began about ten years ago on our Rocklin High School campus, and the results are disheartening in every way.

YouTube, Facebook and Twitter were all available to users by 2006.[58] They quickly became widespread and user friendly, hence the social media era was born. Even more studies have been conducted on the impact of social media on adolescents and teenagers than have been done on the effects of screen time and the results are equally, if not more, devastating.[59] Cyberbullying, sexting, depression and anxiety are all clear results of social media. Combine the use of cell phones with the unrelenting pull of social media on a high school campus and you can guess the outcome...*disastrous*. I did quite a bit of research on my own

---

[58]https://www.huffingtonpost.com/suren-ramasubbu/influence-of-social-media-on-teenagers

[59] http://ourwhitehouse.org/historical-literacy-statistics/

time, and compiled a very concise document of its findings. I sent this to our superintendent, voicing my concerns about changing the district wide cell phone policy in class, and asking for some potential help and clarity regarding how this issue might harmfully affect our students. I never received a reply; not even an acknowledgement of receipt. Very disappointing. (I did not realize it then, of course, because I had no idea that a few years later I would be placed on leave by this same group of administrators; but lack of engagement seems to be their preferred method of how to deal with issues.)

When I posed my questions, and raised my concerns regarding the use of cell phones in class to my colleagues, there was also little support. A very small group of us teachers have firmly resisted the use of cell phones and computers on our campus, and still do so to this day. I was genuinely surprised that there was limited pushback to altering the long-held cell phone policy on campus. A few even chimed in to respond to my concerns, "What is the big deal? What are you afraid of?" In my mind, I murmured: I'll tell you exactly what I'm afraid of: *disengagement.* It is difficult enough for a student to focus and navigate through the incredible peer pressures on a high school campus, but now we're going to allow their world of technology, social media, texting, etc. into the classroom? This is *insane.* And insane it has been ever since.

Amid incredible pressure from the "technology teachers" on campus, our school quickly became a "hotwire" campus with broadband WiFi readily available. And the cell phone policy that required students to keep their cell phones in their backpacks at all times during class was now altered: it was now up to "the individual teacher's discretion on what cell phone rules to have in their particular class." Although this sounds somewhat liberating and appears to promote academic freedom on the part of the teacher, it was ambiguous and murky, neither of which turned out positive. It is vital and necessary to have concrete rules in place on a school campus; if a uniform policy is nonexistent for any issue, then teacher is pitted against teacher and things become incredibly blurred: If one teacher allows free use of cell phones in their class and then another teacher does not, students are confused and are sent mixed messages on proper procedures and guidelines. It also creates a culture of "cool, hip teacher versus strict, out-of-date teacher." A teacher's reputation is everything they have, something they work incredibly hard to earn, and because I was not falling in line with the "cell phone trend" on our campus, I felt, once again, a bit ostracized.

To maintain the classroom environment that I had long enjoyed, I drew a hard line on cell phone use in my class: I bought a shoe hanger with 30 different slots and hung it in my classroom. Students were to place their phone in a slot upon arrival to class. If I found it out in class, then a referral slip was given with two hours of detention attached. This felt very juvenile and punitive to me, because I could not remember the last time that I had issued a citation; there was never a reason for me to do so. But, in this case I didn't know of any other way to ensure that cell phones would not become a distraction in class. Students generally followed my "rules" for the first few weeks of school and then slowly but surely, I would look over to the shoe slots and see less and less phones were being placed there. So now my task was to be on the "lookout" for students who were using them; not a way I wanted to spend my instruction time *at all*. And because students are incredibly clever, they found ways to use their phones without me really seeing them do so. For example, placing their backpacks on their desk and putting the phone underneath to use when I turned away. Or putting them in their coat pocket, out of my sight but close enough for them to reach. As I'm trying to lead a discussion or debate, and notice a student on their phone, I have to make choice: it's not obvious to anyone but me that this student is on their phone because they are being sneaky about it. But I know they are using it so I have two options... call them out, confiscate the phone, assign them a referral and embarrass them in front of the whole class, or ignore them and betray my conscience. Neither option is ideal, and I have chosen the first on several occasions but it gets tiresome and weary; so, more times than not I opt for the latter: Ignore the cell phone use and try to continue to engage with the remaining students who are abiding by the rules.

The school year starts in August and by mid-February, there are about 2-3 cell phones left in my shoe slot. Multiple students are now discreetly on their phones, and I am exhausted from the fight...*why are we even here?* I sometimes asked myself. Snapchat stories and the latest trending videos are so much more appealing and desirable to this generation than reading MLK Jr.'s *Letter from A Birmingham Jail.* My heart is grieved. But press on I shall, so as a class we read aloud this beautiful document that eloquently addresses the critics who suggested that the Civil Rights Movement and its leaders were pushing too far and needed to be more patient. As an instructor, I feel good every time we read a primary source aloud and dissect its historical context and meaning; these students are understanding the brilliance and beauty embedded here, correct? I certainly hope so. But as soon as the bell rings to dismiss, or if I close out a minute or two before class ends, students immediately default to their cell phones. Heads down, fingers churning, back in their cyber world. Little to no engagement with those around them, and they care even less. Sigh.

The next suggestion on our campus was to get "google chrome books and ipads available for every student!" Good night, I responded only to myself in my head again...where does this end? "We are in the 21st century so our students need to be technologically literate if they're going to compete in the real world," they continued. Yikes. I offered the following in response, "Literate? How about having our students read an actual *book*? Why are we sticking another screen in their face? And what is so wrong with a pencil and paper?" The ensuing tension that I have often felt while in these discussions was again paramount. I will not waste your time with the obvious complexity of how to administer an exam on a Chromebook or Ipad; these suggestions were not well thought out, in my estimation. The google server does not "lock" and it would therefore be far too easy and tempting for a student to open up a new tab during the test to look up the answers. A teacher would have to "hover" over every kid on test day, which is absolutely impractical with a class of 35 students.

I find it utterly fascinating and simultaneously frightening, that the Silicon Valley technocrats, who shove this technology into our public school system (there are 4 levels to becoming a "google certified Educator"...Woo Hoo!) send their own kids to Waldorf schools, where screens of any kind are flatly prohibited. As the *New York Times* article explains,

"The chief technology officer of eBay sends his children to a nine-classroom school here. So do employees of Silicon Valley giants like Google, Apple, Yahoo and Hewlett-Packard. But the school's chief teaching tools are anything but high-tech: pens and paper, knitting needles and, occasionally, mud. Not a computer to be found. No screens at all. They are not allowed in the classroom, and the school even frowns on their use at home. The Waldorf method is nearly a century old, but its foothold here among the digerati puts into sharp relief an intensifying debate about the role of computers in education. "[60]

Throughout our nation's history, there has *always* been a stratification between the ruling class and the rest of us ordinary, common folk. First, we saw it with the Plantocracy: the Southern Elite and their slaves. After the civil war, we saw the emergence of the Plutocracy: the Industrial Elite and their workers. Today, we have what I will call the Snobocracy: (Historians will ascribe a more sophisticated, nuanced label in due time.) Hollywood Actors, Media Icons, Ivy Tower Academia, and the Technology Executives. These same people who push their violent narratives through film and music, deride Trump's policies at every opportunity, and indoctrinate our students with their prescribed ideology,

[60]https://www.nytimes.com/2011/10/23/technology/at-waldorf-school-in-silicon-valley-technology-can-wait.html

are the same ones who don't allow their own kids to watch television or own iphones. They lament the building of the "Border Wall" and the 2nd amendment, while they live carefree in their million-dollar fortresses that cannot even be seen from the road, protected with armed guards. Incredulous.

It is well documented that civic and historical literacy is at an all-time low. David McCullough, a prolific author and historian, of whose work I have read every one, (yes, he is just that good!) writes with great concern that, "I think we are raising a generation of young Americans who are, to a very large degree, completely unaware of their past."[61] Understanding the basic functionality of our democracy and knowing our nation's past is the responsibility of all citizens. Perhaps the most glaring example of an uninformed electorate is that "One in five Americans (21 percent) incorrectly thinks that a 5-4 Supreme Court decision is sent back to Congress for reconsideration, 35% of Americans could not name one single branch of the government, and when asked about the significance of Normandy, 67% did not know why there was an American cemetery there."[61] A free, democratic society cannot afford such ignorance. The stunning obsession with 28-year old Alexandria Ocasio-Cortez is a borderline bench mark of where we are at; although she is darling and

[61] http://ourwhitehouse.org/historical-literacy-statistics/

enthusiastic, her limited knowledge of basic concepts is disconcerting, to say the least. 71% of millennials do not understand what socialism actually entails, and yet her platform to sell it to the nation is gaining traction at an alarming rate. As a recent article suggests, "The 28-year-old candidate advocates for guaranteed federal jobs, free college for all, Medicare for all, and the abolishment of the Immigration and Customs Enforcement (ICE) agency. She'd like to turn Uncle Sam into Santa Claus, handing out freebies 365 days a year – all paid for by crushing taxes on all of us, a skyrocketing national debt or … hey, whatever." [62] She is a glaring example of public education gone awry.

And so it goes...on most of our public school campuses, classic education is not the norm at all. The push for "Career Paths" and "Technological Trades" is all the buzz right now. It's highly important and should be encouraged that we develop new programs and options for students to excel and achieve in fields that they are naturally interested in, but to leave behind the beauty and grit of all those who created this nation and allowed it to stabilize and then flourish, is a grave injustice to the past. I have some wonderful British friends with whom I thoroughly enjoy conversing with any time we get the chance to visit. What I am struck by, particularly from my time spent in England and the European continent as

[62] https://www.dailywire.com/news/38028/ocasio-cortez-gop-hasnt-earned-right-ask-how-ill-ryan-saavedra

a whole, is how well versed the *average* citizen is in history, politics, and current events. And not just about their own nation's history but about America's. I would venture to say that the majority of Europeans know more about the United States' past and present affairs than do the majority of Americans. I find this both alarming and disheartening. Our American culture is vibrant and exciting but far too many are focused on the here and now, and could care less about what happened before they were alive. David Crabtree of Gutenberg College states it best when he argues:

> History is important. In centuries past this statement would have seemed self-evident. Ancient cultures devoted much time and effort to teaching their children family history. It was thought that the past helps a child understand who he is. Modern society, however, has turned its back on the past. We live in a time of rapid change, a time of progress. We prefer to define ourselves in terms of where we are going, not where we come from. Our ancestors hold no importance for us. They lived in times so different from our own that they are incapable of shedding light on our experience. Man is so much smarter now than he was even ten years ago that anything from the past is outdated and irrelevant to us. Therefore, the past, even the relatively recent past, is, in the minds of most of us, enshrouded by mists and only very vaguely perceived. Our ignorance of the past is not the result of a lack of information, but of indifference. We do not believe that history matters. But history does matter. It has been said that he who controls the past controls the future. Our view of history shapes the way we view the present, and therefore it dictates what answers we offer for existing problems.[63]

It's not just history, however. Other subjects in school are seeing less and less success rates, and our academic achievement on a global scale

---

[63] http://msc.gutenberg.edu/2001/02/the-importance-of-history/
[64] http://www.pewresearch.org/fact-tank/2017/02/15/u-s-students-internationally-math-science/

is less than admirable. American students are in the "middle of the pack in science, math and reading scores compared to other industrialized nations in the world."[64] The same Pew Research poll found that the much-touted STEM program (Science, Technology, Engineering and Math) was considered the "best or above average" by just 16% and in contrast, 46% said K-12 STEM in the U.S. was below average. We clearly have some work to do to change these downward trends in our educational system. The recent opening of the "I Promise School" in Akron, Ohio is a potential blueprint for the education makeover that needs to occur in this country.[65] A much needed discussion must begin. Until then, public schools should begin each year by adopting Dennis Prager's "Important Changes Coming" speech which provides imperative suggestions on how to honor and unite all students and members of a school community.[66]

Am I blaming all school issues on the use of cell phones and google chrome books in class? Of course not. But allowing students unlimited and undisciplined access to their phones and computers during a school day adds up to at least five more hours per day that they are on a device, when they can and should be engaged in a rich and challenging curriculum, genuinely collaborating with their peers and teachers. The

[65] http://time.com/money/5354265/lebron-james-i-promise-school-akron
[66] https://www.nationalreview.com/2010/07/real-education-dennis-prager
[67] https://www.theguardian.com/education/2015/may/16/schools-mobile-phones-

research is quite conclusive: schools that ban cell phone use see better academic and social success among their students.[67]

V. Hello There, Abigail

"Daughter! Get you an honest Man for a Husband, and keep him honest. No matter whether he is rich, provided he be independent. Regard the Honour and moral Character of the Man more than all other Circumstances. Think of no other Greatness but that of the soul, no other Riches but those of the Heart. An honest, Sensible humane Man."

-John Adams

I admire and revere Abigail Adams immensely. She and I have much in common. She was a mere 5 ft. tall and I "tower" over her by only a few more inches. She had five kids, so do I. She respected and adored her husband. Ditto. A mere glance through the love letters exchanged between John and Abigail Adams demonstrates a sincere and mutual admiration for one another. It is a common held belief that Abigail was her husband's most trusted and sought after political confidante.[68] May I humbly suggest that we could use a few more political marriages like the one John and Abigail shared?

I am the last person who will "preach" to you about marriage. I was a very lost and insecure young woman, who at the age of 19 married a good and decent man who was 27. What was I thinking? I have no idea. I

---

[68] My Dearest Friend: Letters of Abigail and John Adams Margaret A. Hogan, ed. & C. James Taylor, 2010

had absolutely no business getting married at the age of 19, especially to someone eight years older than me. The disparity between someone who had just graduated high school the year before and someone who is almost 30 and well into his career is quite remarkable. It happened very quickly and ended very quickly. I was selfish, immature, and should never have been able to make such a rash decision.

But I did make it and I do own it. The heartbreak that followed my one year of marriage was startling. I was divorced at the age of 21. Wow, that was never in the plan! The stigma alone was almost too much to bear. I felt like a failure and that things would never be the same again. I really wanted a thriving marriage with a genuine partner who was my best friend. Now I felt that I had missed my opportunity and would probably have to settle for less than best. Boy, was I wrong.

The first 25 years of my life were very typical and average. Born into a middle-class family, there wasn't anything exceptional or spectacular with how we lived. My dad is a very intelligent engineer who was a great provider for our family: gender roles in the 1970s were being challenged but still firmly in place. My mom stayed at home to take care of my sister and me, and she never felt demeaned or less than for doing so. We took wonderful family vacations to British Columbia, the Santa Barbara Islands, Yosemite National Park, Death Valley, and so on. We mostly camped in tents or sailed on a rented 40-foot vessel so adventure was always at the top of the list.

But like many of us out there, without a firm foundation in Christ, I really did not have a keen sense and confidence in who I was as a person. Desperately searching through my adolescence and teenage years, I tried to fill the void that was clearly missing in my life. I came up short every time. It wasn't until I was 25 years of age that I reached a place of total and complete surrender to the Creator of the Universe. I vividly recall after driving home from a Sunday night prayer service pulling into a random parking lot, my heart overwhelmed and my eyes filled with tears. I proclaimed to God that, "I am tired of trying to control and dictate my own life. I've done a crummy job, and if you are willing to pick up the shambles of the mess that I have made, I am completely yours." It was truly a life-altering prayer that fundamentally *transformed* who I was, and I have never, ever looked back.

What I did not anticipate was the thrill ride that God had in store for me once I surrendered my life completely. Within that year, by the time I turned 26, I was hired to teach at Rocklin High School, and I simultaneously met the *true* love of my life, who was already a teacher on campus, and a very attractive one at that. We both went to "See You at the Pole," which is a nationwide event where students pray for their schools at

7:15 am, appropriately thirty minutes *before* the class bell rings. It was destiny, to say the least. He called me that night and our first date was the following week. With a much clearer head on my shoulders, and a ton of real life experience to help guide my decision, we were married on April 3, 1998.

Do I represent the best of America? Not even close. But my husband? Yes, he certainly does. In fact, once you meet him, you'll want him to run for President instead of me, but that's too bad. I filed, he didn't. I am perhaps better suited for the job - a little feisty and salty. That's surely needed, right? Born and raised in the San Francisco Bay Area, I am a little more rough around the edges than my husband. Greg Benzel *is* the best of America. Born in Lincoln, CA into a very blue collar family, his dad served in the Air Force during Vietnam and then became the grounds crew supervisor for a local school district. My husband was the first of four siblings to attend and graduate with a college degree. He sees the best in everything and everyone. He adheres more to the Rousseauian view of human nature and I am a Hobbesian at heart. He adores our five daughters and has invested his time and energy into their development. It is breathtaking.

He stuck to his principles and saved himself for marriage; this was a gift that I did not deserve. And yet that is the beauty of Amazing Grace, isn't it? We get what we never *should* have, and we are forgiven of the egregious errors we have made. My husband was a genuine Godsend to me, and I made a personal vow that I would never take for granted or advantage of this incredible second chance that I was given. That has not always been an easy vow to keep, however. The cultural pull to try to get "ahead" of men certainly has been intense. Respect and revere your husband? It almost seemed like a foreign concept to many of my female friends.

This cultural shift had already been turning since the 1970's feminist challenge to traditional gender roles. By the 1990s, it was in full force and the landscape of the American marriage and family was certainly changing. By 2010, the Pew Research Center conducted an exhaustive study titled, "The Decline of Marriage and Rise of New Families." The results clearly demonstrated that the concept of a life-long partner and what constituted the familial structure had indeed been altered.[69] Perhaps the following excerpt from the study sums it up best:

☐ **Changing Spousal Roles.** In the past 50 years, women have reached near parity with men as a share of the workforce and have begun to outpace men in educational attainment. About six-in-ten

---

[69] http://www.pewsocialtrends.org/2010/11/18/the-decline-of-marriage-and-rise-of-new-families

wives work today, nearly double the share in 1960. There's an unresolved tension in the public's response to these changes. More than six-in-ten (62%) survey respondents endorse the modern marriage in which the husband and wife both work and both take care of the household and children; this is up from 48% in 1977. Even so, the public hasn't entirely discarded the traditional male breadwinner template for marriage. Some 67% of survey respondents say that in order to be ready for marriage, it's very important for a man to be able to support his family financially; just 33% say the same about a woman. These dramatic changes in the economic status of women have had wide-ranging effects on family structure. In the 1950s and 1960s, most married women did not work outside the home, instead relying on their husbands' income to support the family. In 1960, 32% of wives were in the labor force. By 2008, that share had risen to 61%.[70]

There you have it. We are in a new era where traditional gender roles have altered and continue to do so. Most of the changes brought about by the feminist movement have been positive gains for women: educational opportunities, workplace equality, shared child and household duties between spouses, job share and flexible scheduling, and the list goes on.[71] I applaud all of those measures and the tenacious women who have

[70] http://www.pewsocialtrends.org/2010/11/18/the-decline-of-marriage-and-rise-of-new-families

fought valiantly for them. But there *are* differences between men and women, and to suggest otherwise is myopic and foolish.

So, let's get back to John and Abigail Adams. Did Abigail have the right to vote (and hence the political equal to men) in the 18th century? Not even close. Was she oppressed, unappreciated, and disrespected by her husband and children? Hardly. Abigail Adams was a fiercely intelligent woman who put her family first, above all else. Was she ridiculed and demeaned for doing so? Not at all. Nor should any woman in the 21st century be so either. Yet it is somewhat par for the course today for women to try to "get ahead" of men, outdo them, prove that they are better than, and so on. Foolishness, absolute foolishness.

A small but principled stand I took in regard to this issue on my high school campus was when a liberal colleague of mine, whose political views were well known because she made them so, sent out an email in honor of "International Women's Day."[72] She wanted to "commend and applaud all of the courageous, bold and beautiful women on our campus for all you are and all you stand for. I cheer you on," she declared. Wait a minute, was my usual thought. As you have probably guessed by now, I question just about everything. What about all of the *men* on our campus, who are working just as diligently on behalf of students? Maybe I should

---

[71] https://learningenglish.voanews.com/a/abigail-adams-feminist-partner-first-lady
[72] https://www.internationalwomensday.com

have resisted but I couldn't; a man certainly would not be able to suggest a counter argument because he would be easily and quickly labeled "sexist," so I sent out an email in response: "International Men's Day was on November 19th[73] and I do not recall an email being sent out? I would therefore like to take this opportunity to applaud all of the courageous, bold and beautiful men on our campus for all you are and all you stand for. I cheer you on." Seemed reasonable to me? Oh boy. Aside from the myriad of men who came by my classroom to offer their thanks and appreciation for my courage, I was condemned elsewhere and told to, "stop using all staff emails for this form of communication." Interesting to note that issues this administration agrees with and condones are deemed valid as a topic over email, but when I open my annoying mouth to suggest an opposing viewpoint, they somehow declare it "inappropriate?" Hmmm.

Back to marriage: Now, I will admit, it has been tempting over the course of 20 years to laugh and banter back and forth with my female friends and colleagues about our husbands. It's our time as women to shine in the sun anyway, right? This is our new era, and men will now have to take a backseat, correct? We women just do everything so much better than men anyway, don't we? I can't count the times I have heard my friends

---

[73] https://www.internationalmensday.com

refer to their husbands as an "additional child," or have witnessed them treat their husbands like they *are* a child. The scorn and ridicule is sometimes endless. How is this healthy or helpful? The answer is: it's not. Women and men are different. [74] And just as we love to celebrate the differences between the races, religions, and creeds, so too should we celebrate those things that make us distinctly male and female.[75] Whether you believe in God as the Creator of the Universe or not, it must be acknowledged that the sexes can and should complement one another. We are not at war with each other.

My husband has unique characteristics and talents that I do not. I have several attributes that he does not possess. Men are typically more concerned with the "big picture" while women like details, details, and more details. Men tend to get singularly focused while many women thrive on multitasking. So be it. When women try to be men, be better than men, or outright condemn men, the result is rarely positive. The trajectory of the feminist movement in the 21st Century has been disappointing, to say the least. They have no clear focus and continue to tout that sexual openness and choice are the greatest avenues to liberty for a woman.[76] Hogwash. How about trying some modesty and restraint? Those attributes lead to *real*, lasting freedom.

[74] https://list25.com/25-biological-differences-between-men-and-women
[75] http://socialistreview.org.uk/340/21st-century-feminism
[76] https://www.washingtonpost.com/wp/2016/06/30/feminists-treat-men-badly-its-bad-

As incredibly wonderful as my husband is, he is not an anomaly. I see the likes of him every day when I bring our three-year old daughter to preschool: other conscientious, engaged, and nurturing men who sincerely love their families and put them first and foremost in their lives. I see hard-working men who use what valuable extra time they have to coach a little league team or serve in the youth group. Men should be applauded, and yet mainstream culture has diminished the impact that they have had and continue to attack them as defenders of a "western civilization patriarchy" who are full of "toxic masculinity." It's laughable. As if most men are sitting around conspiring on how to keep women oppressed and void of any further progress. Give me a break.

I am genuinely weary of hearing how everything is man's fault, particularly white men. The "revisionist" historians of the late 1960s and early 1970s[77], whose savior came by way of Howard Zinn and his publication, *A People's History of the United States*, portrays a side of American history that can largely be seen as the exploitation and manipulation of the majority by rigged systems that hugely favor a small aggregate of elite rulers from across the orthodox political parties.[78] Ugh. Almost every "white man" in history has been demonized because of their

for-feminism
[77]https://news.stanford.edu/news/2012/december/wineburg-historiography-zinn-122012.html
[78] Zinn, Howard. *A People's History of the United States.* New York: Harper Collins, 1980.

egregious sins of living in their prescribed century: Christopher Columbus is now considered a "murderous moron who was a doofus at math."[79] Wow.

And to prove how far this has come, Sarah Jeong just got hired at the *New York Times* even after ugly and horrific tweets about white men were unearthed.[80] Not only are people writing in her defense, but they seem genuinely shocked that some would suggest she should not be hired; unequivocally, if a white man went on a hating rant over Twitter about an Asian woman, I am quite certain that the NYT would consider him wholly disqualified. This is yet another explicit and disheartening example of the incessant double standard. It gets tiresome, doesn't it?

Although I am not a Factual Feminist because I disagree with her stance on abortion, I applaud Christina Hoff Sommers and her voracious and tireless work to "debunk false claims and erroneous statistics to promote a misleading agenda regarding women." [81] As a conservative feminist (which I offer is the best kind of feminist), I vow to uphold the integrity and honor of manhood. And marriage in general; it can and should be a beautiful covenant where there is mutual respect and

---

[79] https://www.vox.com/identities/2017/10/9/16447180/christopher-columbus-day-adam-ruins-everything
[80] https://money.cnn.com/2018/08/02/media/new-york-times-sarah-jeong-twitter/index.html
[81] https://www.aei.org/feature/factual-feminist

admiration. We saw this portrayed over 200 years ago with John and Abigail Adams, and it is healthy and prudent to promote it today. One sex does not need to dominate the other in any capacity, but the unique strengths of one another should be celebrated. As wives, we must stand against the cultural pressure to outdo them or constantly compete with them. A mutually respectful partnership is attainable in the 21st century. My husband is one incredible man. We have made decisions regarding our careers, family and future together. We wholeheartedly agreed as a family unit to file with the FEC to run for POTUS. Not only will my husband be the greatest pioneer for the role of First Man, but he will unequivocally be my most trusted political confidante. I think Abigail would be proud.

VI. The Beauty of Being Unseen

"He who is not a good servant will not be a good master."

-Plato

Almost immediately after I announced that I was running for President of the United States, the common reaction was, "This is the greatest news I have heard in a long time; just what our country needs right now; you would be a breath of fresh air; so inspiring; you can do it." But there were, of course, some detractors, and understandably so: "Um, who do you think you are? POTUS? Do you really think you're qualified? Perhaps you should run for the school board, city council, state assembly, or congress? You're going for the big prize right out of the gate? That's just silly." Or yet another, "Do you really think you're going to trump Trump?" To which I kindly responded, "I have no idea; 2020 is two years away. We are simply building our campaign, one day at a time. But I *do* trust the American people to elect whom they think will best represent them. What *must* continue is the Populist movement that Trump ushered in with his election. And it is *high time* for a woman to emerge on the

Republican national ticket. The Left has hijacked the female narrative for far too long."

I genuinely respect the critics who suggest that I should take the "necessary steps" to becoming a political candidate: "George Bush started out as a member of city council. Take it slow, be realistic, use your clout where it can do the most good, this is an obvious overreach," and on and on, they proclaim. I get it. But this is what the critics don't understand: I am not a politician and I did not plan for any of this to happen. It would make perfect sense, and be genuinely logical, for me to start out on the local or statewide level to embark on this new journey as a candidate. Agreed. But nothing that has happened to me in the last six months has made sense and been logical in any way.

Even the most thoughtful and well-meaning friends have suggested, "David was a shepherd in the wilderness for 30 years before he slayed Goliath. The Israelites wandered in the desert for 40 years before they reached the Promised Land. Jesus was a carpenter for 30 years before he began his ministry that altered the course of human history." Agreed on all accounts. Perhaps like Noah, whom God told to build a giant boat in the middle of a wilderness where it had *never* rained before, we are building a campaign that looks foolish from the outside, but we are genuinely following where we believe God is leading us. May I add another biblical reference to this list that might help explain my situation? The story of Esther.

Let me be clear that I do not think I am a "brave and beautiful young Queen called by God to save her people," which is how Esther is usually referred.[82] The part I would like to draw your attention to is how Esther was an *ordinary* woman who was living a humble and rather *plain* life when God decided to pluck her out of obscurity and drop her into the grandest palace to have the greatest influence on the most powerful man in the world at the time. Esther was a nobody until King Xerxes I chose her to be his wife. She found the boldness and courage to approach him, even though she was risking her life to do so.[83]

Am I suggesting that I am risking my life as Esther did? Not hardly. I perhaps am risking my reputation, since there are surely more critics out there who think I am wholly unworthy and unqualified to be POTUS, but I don't mind. I can handle the ridicule that will undoubtedly ensue. What I would like to suggest is that I *have* spent my life preparing, perhaps in ways that are unorthodox for a likely presidential candidate, but I hope you will at least consider them.

---

[82] http://www.womeninthebible.net/women-bible-old-new-testaments/esther-story

[83] http://www.womeninthebible.net/women-bible-old-new-testaments/esther-story

I never once in my life thought that I would be a candidate for *any* government position. As noted in previous chapters, I have been thoroughly engaged and passionate about the political process since I was 14 years old, but that does not translate into desiring to be elected to office. Nothing could have been further from my mind. Even when my students, year after year, suggested that I run for POTUS, I never gave it even a remote consideration. They just want a better grade, and are hoping flattery will work, was my thought (which was probably correct in most cases).

But, just as the examples of David and Jesus in the Bible were servants, so too have I lived a servant's life. (Please do not misinterpret me; I am not comparing myself to Jesus, nor do I think I am *anything* close to him, but his *example* is what I am referring to). The teaching profession alone is a unique and selfless calling and most educators are genuinely in it because of a sincere love and desire to serve their students. That was certainly my motivation. I have poured my heart and soul into what I have always referred to as my "darling" students. Rocklin is a fairly affluent city, whose average family has resources and access to opportunities, so I have taught some of the most talented minds in this country. I have always applauded and cheered them on, continued relationships with them well after high school, was genuinely excited to see what would become of their futures and was confident that I would be voting for one of *them* to become POTUS at some point in my life.

I have volunteered in the toddler room at my church for the past *twenty* years every other Sunday: changing dirty diapers, wiping snotty noses, and holding crying babies for over an hour so their parents could enjoy the sermon; I've led a small group of preteen girls, ages 8-11 every Wednesday night to help them on life's journey; served on the Board of Directors for Destiny Christian Church and then Destiny Community Center. I am proud to say that while on the Board of Directors we made a very courageous and bold decision to open a Community Center with the sole purpose to "Love Our City." And we did just that: free after school tutoring programs, single and blended family parenting classes, a Bike & Toy Giveaway at Christmas time for underprivileged kids in the greater Sacramento area, a Backpack Giveaway in August before school started to give not only backpacks, but shoes, clothes, haircuts, and any other essential items necessary to start the school year right; and possibly the greatest gift of all to our community: Celebrate America. This is an outdoor event with live music, vendors, kids play areas, booths to support local vendors, local politicians in attendance and speaking, a beautiful tribute to our military veterans, and perhaps the best part of all: an aerial fireworks show that is top rate. My husband and I also led a "married with kids" small group who met every other Saturday night to eat, pray and encourage one another on life's journey. This is what we have spent the last two decades of our lives doing.

I will stop there because I don't want it to appear that I have been some kind of martyr who has given her entire life to help others. Not at all. But I *have* served. And I have served *faithfully*. I have never questioned it nor sought to get anything out of it. It just seemed like the right thing to do and the best way to use my life, and I am not unusual. There are millions out there just like me who diligently help others, day in and day out.

Let me reiterate how unbelievably ordinary and common I am. To affirm this notion, I took heed when my pastor declared recently in a sermon, "God does not call the qualified, he qualifies the called." And as I peruse through my Bible, I do quickly notice that God seems to choose the most basic and average people to do extraordinary things. There is certainly something powerful about being a servant. Jesus demonstrated it best in John 13:1-17 when he washed his disciple's feet. Humbling oneself might just be the greatest attribute of a leader after all?

Please don't mistake me: there isn't anything wrong with ambition per se, but our culture certainly pulls and tugs at you from all directions to "climb the ladder of success, strive for greatness, put yourself and your needs first, you can do it." I'm just not sure this is the best strategy to live by. Isn't there something refreshing and altogether beautiful about someone who thinks less of themselves and more about others? I know it's certainly tempting to give in and live for yourself and your own goals; to resist and take a stand against this is certainly not easy. But from my experience in serving for 20 years, it's also extremely liberating. Perhaps my thirty years of analyzing American history has brought me to a place of peace knowing that plenty of others have gone before us and plenty others will come after; we are but mere dust in the wind, really. What does all of it matter anyway if we have not given of our time, money and resources for a cause outside of ourselves?

And my 20 years of serving have not been dreadful by any means. It's been beautiful "behind the scenes." Much like David as he tended his sheep, there are valuable lessons to be learned when no one is noticing or seems to care. It is most commonly stated that "crisis builds character," but I would like to suggest that "crisis *reveals* character," it does not create it. What you have been doing in the desert for 20, 30, or 40 years is who you *really* are; the day in and day out mundane tasks of ordinary life matter immensely. The relationships you build, how you use your resources, and the way you spend your time all total the sum of who you are.

I see servanthood every day: The grandparents picking up their grand kids from preschool so both parents can work. The single mom and dad juggling and rearranging their schedules to meet the needs of their children. The janitors and secretaries at local schools, who are by far the most important, yet humble people on campus. The special education aides who tend to one student for the entire day so those who are disabled can participate in a somewhat normal school experience. The nurses who took care of me after delivering my babies are absolute saints in every way. Oh, and the stay-at-home moms and dads, whom I refer to as "angels on earth," who give up practically all of their own personal ambition to tend to the needs of their family. Admirable and inspiring.

And yet this is the fabric of American life: the totality of everyday heroes, doctors, police, firefighters, military personnel, search and rescue teams; I could go on and on. We have plenty of unsung heroes and we need to shine a spotlight on their everyday contributions more often to reinforce the *beauty of the ordinary*. And then there comes an occasional moment in everyone's life when the ordinary steps out to do something extraordinary. Here's a quick glimpse of when our "unseen lives" garnered a little more attention than we anticipated.

"All politics is local" you have surely heard it said. And it is certainly true. The criticism that I don't have any experience and that I should take minor steps on my road to the White House is understandable. But may I offer what I consider to be one of my greatest political accomplishments to date? Let me provide a brief pretext first: When my husband and I found out we were having a surprise baby, one of our first thoughts was, "where are we going to put her?" We literally had no other room in our small and humble track home. We found a beautiful house in one of the more upscale neighborhoods in Rocklin called Whitney Oaks. Never in our wildest dreams did we think we would ever live there, but a house was for sale whose price had dropped substantially, to a level we could actually afford. We were thrilled beyond belief because it backed up to the high school where my husband and I both taught and our oldest daughter was about to be a freshman. We could all walk back and forth to school since we're there multiple times throughout the day. Perfect.

The first year came and went without a hitch. There was a beautiful little path that went from our neighborhood right to the high school campus, with a precious little creek running alongside that almost filled to the brim on a rainy day. Are we living in utopia, we thought? This was just too wonderful. Our cars sat in the driveway 90% of the time. Life was good; really, really good. But the next year was fundamentally different. I recall getting the message on the Saturday night before school was going to start that the school had erected a barbed wire fence and the walking path was no longer accessible.

Hogwash, was my initial response. And then came the obvious question...why would they do this? We sought answers immediately but they were slow to come. Whose idea was this to block the walking path access? The back and forth exchange between the "powers that be" was enough to make one dizzy, but the end result we eventually discovered was that our Home Owner's Association had pressured the high school to put the fence up. Why, we wondered? So, we sought more answers. We attended the monthly HOA Board meetings for *over a year* trying to get to the bottom of this issue - inquiring, researching, and developing proposals of our own. I personally walked the neighborhood, knocking on doors and acquiring signatures for a petition to get the path reopened. We presented this all to the HOA Board but what did we get in return? Contempt and disdain from the Board President and her sidekick, the Board Secretary. We were new to a "gated community and homeowner's association" neighborhood and nothing could have prepared us for that following year.

Having done our due diligence, spending an enormous amount of time on this issue of allowing students and staff to *walk to school*, we realized the obstinance of the HOA Board president was essentially the roadblock to any progress. She was quite a bit older and had been in her position for over 10 years; no one ever challenged or questioned her before... *until now*. We tried to be nice, but it got us nowhere. Her comments toward us at the board meetings were condescending and disdainful. It appeared that she did not like teenagers because she lumped them all into a "troublesome kind who will engage in illicit behavior on that walking path if we continue to allow access to it." There had not been one reported (or unreported) incident of any mischievous activities on what was no more than a 50-foot pathway to the school campus.

Although we attempted to "adjust" and drove to school a couple times, it violated our conscience to the point that we simply could not do it any longer. We were driving through 3 stop signs and 5 stop lights, sitting in 15-20 minutes of jam-logged, morning traffic (and that was just one way) to get around to a campus that we could literally see from our yard. That year was hard, *really hard.* We opted to take the only other route to get to school which was a further walk around, but in actuality I would describe it as more of a *trek.* Instead of navigating on the original path that was now closed, we climbed a rather steep incline to get to the top of a ridge that flattened out and then descended onto the high school campus. It was much less convenient, but you can always find a silver lining, right? Our heart rate and blood flow increased significantly every day on this new, more arduous route, and we enjoyed butterflies, jack rabbits, and wild turkeys along the way. We purchased some heavy, durable shoes once the weather started to change since we refused to relent, and persisted through the rain, mud and cold during the bitter winter months. I literally felt like Laura Ingles Wilder from *Little House on the Prairie*. (I had always thought it would be nostalgic to live in the 19th century and for a year of my life, I knew what it was like, in some regard.)

No progress had been made in over a year so we decided to take action. We had been amiable and patient but that was all about to end. Why? Because the November Board elections were coming up and guess whose term was up? Yup. The Board president had to campaign for her position and I guarantee she never anticipated what would ensue within the next few months. Starting in July, a group of four families who were passionately devoted to this cause came to our house for a strategy meeting. We aired out the big issues and sought ways to not only oust the President but get our candidates elected.

It was a long meeting that night and there were several others that followed. Tedious and tiring, yes. Don't forget that in the midst of all of this, we are still working at our jobs, my husband is coaching football, we are raising five kids, attending ball games and volunteering at church, so extra time was an extremely valuable asset that we really did not have. But some things in life are worth taking a stand for, and the ability of kids to walk to school was most definitely one of them. We were relentless. The same four families spent our own money on lawn signs, and spread them throughout the vast acreage of the entire Whitney Oaks neighborhood. My daughters and I personally put chocolate and "vote for" slips into plastic bags and, together with the four families, placed them on every single door step in this entire complex, which consists of over 5,000 people in over 1,850 homes.[84] I had never been on social media before but everyone insisted that the NextDoor App was an essential and effective tool for our campaign. They were right.

The week of the elections in mid-November we purchased red, white, and blue balloons with a "vote" message attached and placed them strategically where they would get the most visibility. Did we face opposition? At the highest level. Our lawn signs were taken twice (found at the local elementary school dumpster by the janitor who was empathetic to our cause and kindly returned them to us), so we immediately stuck them back in the yards. The HOA Board meeting that month was more heated than before, garnering even local media coverage. As a result, some of the comments on social media by the Board President were ruthless and shocking, to say the least. But when the election was over and the votes were tallied, we prevailed, and did so by a very wide margin. The president was dethroned, the other board members were in shock and now clearly on

---

[84] www.whiteyoaks.net

alert, and one of our candidates was ushered in. Ahhh.... the sheer sense of satisfaction.

The results? We can once again enjoy a beautiful stroll along the path as we walk to the high school campus. Silly? *No way*. There is nothing more intrusive than an HOA Board telling you what to do, where you can park, what color you can paint your house, how much they will raise your dues, and whether you can walk to school or not. My family, along with a few extremely dedicated neighbors, invoked a grassroots strategy to take out a 10-year "establishment" president who ruled arbitrarily and whose decisions were never challenged before we fomented what I consider to be one of the most successful campaigns in the history of local politics. Job well done, thank you.

Was it worth it? Absolutely. We could have easily given up, and many times we wanted to, but we didn't. Even at the behest of many people who suggested, "why don't you just drive your car around to school?" Why on earth should we? It was purely nonsensical to get in our cars and drive through five stop lights that took us over 20 minutes due to traffic congestion to get to a campus that we could literally see from our yard. A stand is a stand, no matter how small. This stand meant *everything* to those families in our neighborhood who wanted and desired to have a quick, easy, and safe path for their kids to *walk* to school. We should be promoting walking to school, correct? Or am I way off base here? Sometimes it's the minor issues that we willingly give in to, when we can fight back if we know we are in the right. Was it easy? Not at all. In fact, far more arduous than we would have ever imagined, and if you would have told me how many hours we would have to invest to put into this two-year campaign, I never would have agreed to do it. I also understand why people don't get engaged in politics or are apathetic. It's a lot of work. But we *must* do it. We cannot relent, cannot give in, cannot be faint hearted when the road is tough. Maintaining steadfast courage in the face of injustice is worth the stand every time.

VII. Trump: The Left Comes Unhinged

Our country finds itself confronted by conditions for which there is not precedent in the history of the world; we believe that the power of government—in other words, of the people—should be expanded as rapidly and as far as the good sense of an intelligent people and the teaching of experience shall justify...

-Populist Party Platform, 1892

Ok, so here we go...the Presidential election of Donald J. Trump and the Left becoming completely unhinged at his Populist victory. I vividly recall on election night watching the results come in. Florida was called in his favor...*really*? I immediately phoned my friend who lives in Tampa and said, "Is what I'm seeing true? Did your state just go for Trump?" "Yes!" she exuberantly shouted back. I got chills...wow, something special might be happening tonight, I thought. And then when Ohio, Wisconsin and Pennsylvania came in, our house erupted and we could hardly contain ourselves. Did he really just pull this off? This might be the greatest upset of all time. I think it surprised even Donald Trump that he had won.

It was genuinely painful to watch the Hillary campaign try to come to terms with what might be happening. The glorious stage in the shape of the United States was supposed to light up when she walked into the middle of it to give her victory speech. It was to be delivered at the Jacob Javits convention center, a building encased by the largest glass ceiling in Manhattan that was going to metaphorically break via computer technology; and the fireworks show set to blaze over the Hudson River, all shut down momentarily.[85] John Podesta walked onto the stage to console their supporters, urging them to "head home to get some sleep and this conversation should continue tomorrow, more votes need to be counted."[85] Oh boy, I recall thinking: they're actually pitching the age old adage that "more votes still need to be counted"? Yikes. Tears were everywhere in that arena and a rather despondent tone; you could almost feel the shock and despair through the airwaves.

And then over to the Trump Headquarters our television screens took us. A completely different atmosphere. Having been engaged with the political process since I was 14-years old, watching my beloved Ronald Reagan get elected twice, I was immediately struck by what was *missing*: not one balloon or piece of confetti dropped at Trump Tower. Not one.[86] I don't presume to know much about Donald Trump per se, but I think it's

[85]https://www.theguardian.com/us-news/2016/nov/09/hillary-clinton-us-election-night-reaction

[86]https://abcnews.go.com/Politics/video/donald-trumps-2016-election-night-victory-speech

[87]https://www.usatoday.com/story/onpolitics/2012/11/08/romney-election-fireworks-website/1692933/

reasonable to state that he enjoys a bit of fanfare, pomp and circumstance, am I right? If he thought he might win, he would have at least ordered up a few "Red, White & Blue" balloons to be dropped, yes? Even Mitt Romney was confident enough that he had to cancel his scheduled firework show when he lost to Obama in 2012. Although statistically it is extremely difficult to unseat a current president, Romney made sufficient plans to celebrate and was genuinely surprised that he did not win. [87]

So, the historic Populist triumph was complete, even though neither Hillary or Trump saw it coming. Nor did the Left, in general. I always wear a red, white and blue lei to school the day after an election, no matter what the outcome, because I continue to stand in awe of our great democracy and the peaceful, orderly transfer of power from one executive to the next; it truly is a remarkable characteristic of this nation, and it's my small little way of showing off my excitement and support for our electoral process. But the next day after this election seemed different on my school campus. Something was odd. It was intangible, but strong enough to know it was there; oh yes, that's it: *utter despair and disdain.* You could almost feel it.

I gave my usual "day after election" speech to all of my classes (the same one I gave when Bush defeated Gore and then Kerry, and Obama defeated McCain and then Romney): "Yesterday was a great day, whether you agree with the results or not. I'm sorry if your candidate did not win. Please do not worry; take heart, and don't threaten secession or that you're going to move to Canada. You'll get another turn in two years to ensure a "check" on this president with the midterm elections, and then another chance in four years to get your candidate in." In all of my 18 years of teaching, up to that point, I had never had much discussion after my little "speech." Maybe a little murmur here or there, or a confident "yes, Mrs. Benzel, we understand," but nothing prepared me for the comments that ensued the day after Trump's election.

My students quipped, "We just elected a misogynistic sexist to the White House." "This country is going to be really bad for Muslims." "Trump is a racist." "I think presidents should only serve one term." And the comments continued relentlessly. They were not *all* disparaging, but a surprising amount of them were and Trump had literally just got elected the day before. "Are we not going to give him a chance?" I asked. "Should we at least wait for the first 100 days before we judge his presidency?" I followed up. The majority of my students were not interested in a genuine dialogue and exchange, to which I was gravely disappointed because discussing the electoral process was far more rewarding and important than many other things that we are mandated to teach. But, I moved on to my day's scheduled lesson on the causes of World War One. Oh well, I thought. I'm at least going to give Trump a chance; everybody deserves a chance, right? And no matter what I personally thought about Trump's comments or his behavior, what intrigued me as a genuine student of history and politics was the Populist pulse and grass roots support with which he was able to harness and win. Remarkable. A businessman, with no political experience, overthrew the heir to the throne, the Clinton Dynasty and Machine. We were in new territory, and I was thrilled to see what lie ahead.

I should not have been so optimistic. Although I understand why some of the vitriol was hurled at Trump during the campaign trail, he seemed to get more than his fair share. True, that is just the way of politics: it's ugly and personal, and certainly not for the faint of heart. Being a new contender on the stage, Trump was unorthodox in his approach and certainly unfiltered with his comments. I think I stand with many Americans when I say that Trump was not my first choice as a candidate; our family rallied around Ben Carson. But as the wide field of candidates began to shrink, the choice became clearer and clearer, yet the salacious comments only seemed to intensify. One of my colleagues at school, a very intelligent and well-respected teacher, actually commented that he thought, "Trump was a fascist like Hitler." Is that so, I thought?

You truly believe that? Because that is quite some claim, I further pondered in my own mind. And his obviously wasn't an original idea, either. Apparently all the "buzz" was that Trump was *worse* than Hitler? Incredulous. What a completely unfounded comment, especially coming from an educator who knows better the atrocities that Hitler committed. That comment was inflicting an incredible disservice to the 6 million Jews who died in Nazi death camps; to compare Trump in this manner was, in my estimation, irresponsible, at best.

And when Trump pulled off the unthinkable and won the election, it ushered in an entirely new phase of the so-called "resistance." As if the Women's March the day after the election wasn't proof enough of the insanity that was about to occur, (never have I seen a group of so-called feminists wear t-shirts that say, "I'm A Nasty Woman." Really? And you're proud of that?), in my world of *true* feminists who genuinely want *great* things for women, being considered "nasty" has never been on our list of aspirations. We are in uncharted territory, I thought. The chaos that ensued by anti-Trump supporters at his inauguration was almost unbearable to watch; they looked like absolute fools screaming and crying as if the world was actually going to end. I'd never seen anything like it in all my years following politics and watching the beautiful transfer of power from one executive to the next. Of course, they ridiculed his speech and braced themselves for Armageddon.[88]

Let's return back to my high school campus now. Anti-Trump comments from students continued to pour in, day after day. I've always maintained an atmosphere of mutual respect, no matter what opinions are spewed in my classroom, but I also hold students accountable for outlandish remarks: "You cannot just say something in here without backing it up with evidence. If you're going to have a salacious opinion on any subject, it must be supported by facts." For instance, I would press my students and inquire, "Please tell me one thing that you know about Trump and his policies that you view as abhorrent?" I received a very sincere question from one darling young girl: "Mrs. Benzel...Trump is going to be really bad for Mexicans; why can't we have open borders?" Rather than denouncing this notion as ridiculous, or unworthy of discussion, I posed a question back to her: "Why do you think Trump's election is going to be really bad for Mexicans? What do you know about open borders, and why do you think they would be a good idea?" As genuine as her question was, she had no idea what Trump's immigration policies actually were, or what "open borders" entailed; she just happened to be a very lovely, the "world is a beautiful place so let's accept anyone and everyone into our country"

[88] https://www.nytimes.com/2017/01/20/us/politics/democrats-boycott-trump-inauguration-day.html

young woman. She unfortunately has listened to oversimplified talking points - perhaps at home or from the mainstream media. But these mere glimpses of Trump's policies were not helpful to intelligent conversations. A genuine dialogue and exchange seemed to lower the temperature in my class a bit, and bring the dynamics of our discussion back to the respectful and amiable tone that I have always enjoyed.

The faculty and staff was an entirely different experience, however. I vividly recall our female vice principal quip on several occasions, berating Trump, thinking she was very savvy for doing so. And then our actual principal, (yes, the same one who put me on administrative leave) joking about the President and using language that I prefer not to print in this book. To which I immediately chimed in, "I'm not going to put up with that for the next four years." The room was dead silent. Another teacher in the room fired back, "That's OK, he'll be impeached by then." To which I returned the favor, "Good, I love Mike Pence." Silence again. Awkward silence. Do I always have to have the last word? Absolutely not. But I refuse to let my place of employment, which is supposed to be a professional environment, become a toxic cesspool of Leftist political persuasions. Please recall that all of these conversations and "stands" on my behalf have taken place in *required* staff meetings with administrators present and as of late, participating. These are not back hall/water cooler topics during break or lunch; those I have purposefully opted out of because the views offered there are even more frank and salacious.

Our principal, appearing quite annoyed but also realizing that *he* started the conversation so therefore he needed to end it, quickly conceded, "You're right. That was unprofessional on my part. I apologize." The room was tense and awkward and I felt, once again, isolated and alone in my thoughts and stance. Am I really the only one who doesn't think insults hurled at our President, no matter who is holding the office, are appropriate in a staff meeting? I know I couldn't have been the only one to think so, but I certainly was the only one who said so. Comments such as these would have been unequivocally condemned if they were about Obama, and I would have felt the exact same way; personal politics do not belong in a professional environment.

Perhaps if you read about or watched the leaked video of the top Google executives absolutely smear Trump after his election you would understand how I felt. A room full of employees is forced to sit through a litany of so-called intelligent bosses, spew their venomous hatred about our newly elected President to everyone in the room. [89] How presumptuous, arrogant and elitist can one group of executives be to force every employee

[89] https://www.dailywire.com/news/35789/watch-google-execs-bash-trump-supporters-want-make-ryan-saavedra

to listen to their left-wing rhetoric? I think it's safe to say that there surely were *some* conservatives in the room, but they probably felt so marginalized and demeaned that they dare not say they voted for Trump lest they be ostracized, or even worse.

Is Trump perfect? Of course not. Are you? Has he said and done some outlandish things in his life? Absolutely. Have you? The ensuing vitriol toward Trump is what bothers me the most. Perhaps Dennis Prager highlighted it best when he admitted, "I was wrong. My opposition to Donald Trump was wrong, in retrospect. I was wrong. I had friends who supported him, and I didn't understand them. I said, "Are you not aware of what he said about John McCain? Isn't that enough to disqualify the guy?" They perceived in him what I did not perceive in him, that these over-the-top statements – as objectionable as the statements themselves may be, and none of them defended the statements – nevertheless, what they perceived was accurate: a man who doesn't give a damn about what the press says about him. That is the only way to govern. It is the only way to advance the principles of conservatism in the United States is to not give a damn. Would I like Donald Trump to have Mitt Romney's temperament, or for that matter Barack Obama's temperament? Yeah. I would like a whole host of things. People are packages. What a president does is more important to me than a president's demeanor." [90] Dennis has a point; we have reached a crossroads in politics where we have to acknowledge the dissonance between a candidate's policies and their personality and are forced to choose which ultimately matters more in the long run.

Before my Stand was revealed to the nation on March 14, 2018, I was already deeply disturbed by how this president was being treated and portrayed. I know he's tough and can handle it, but it seemed to cross a line that I didn't even know existed. When a supposed comedian (I won't even acknowledge her name because I don't want it printed in my book) holds up a bloodied, severed head of Trump and thinks it's funny, I thought to myself, "What is happening in this country? This is disgusting and extremely disturbing." If you don't like Trump, that's fine. No one is forcing you to do so. But the venomous hatred that has been hurled at him is something I have never witnessed before, ever. It was crude and outlandish.

And why such hatred anyway? Are we so outraged at Trump's moral "failures" that we can't give him a second chance? Sure, I'd prefer an executive who leads with moral propriety and has a fairly clean record to prove it. But we are in the 21st Century and unfortunately the dynamics of who we elect in office have drastically changed. *Or have they?* FDR was more notoriously unfaithful to Eleanor than even JFK was to

[30]https://www.realclearpolitics.com/video/2018/01/28/dennis_prager_i_was_wrong_don ald_trump_is_a_great_president.html

101

Jacqueline. Richard Nixon annihilated any trust and credibility that Americans had toward their Chief Executive. And although Reagan worked tirelessly to restore some decency and dignity to the nation's highest elected office, which was completely shattered with Bill Clinton: an affair with an intern *inside* the oval office...this can't be real, I remember thinking, as the story broke in January 1998.[91] But it was real. Far too real. And the denial that ensued: who could possibly forget the mantra played over and over and over... "I did not have sexual relations with that woman, Ms. Lewinsky." Words that have haunted Bill Clinton ever since. He finally admitted to the affair and was impeached by the House but did not get the ⅔ vote in the Senate to move toward trial and removal from office.[92] I find it insulting that Hillary has tried to become the hero of the #MeToo Movement, but she was nowhere to be found when the voluminous amount of women who accused her husband of sexual assault came forward, including a 21 year old intern. Oh wait, that's right, I forgot...she *did* comment about them: "they're looney, narcissists, and deranged," she said.[93] Monica Lewinsky's life was utterly destroyed as she

---

[91] http://time.com/5120561/bill-clinton-monica-lewinsky-timeline

[92] http://time.com/5120561/bill-clinton-monica-lewinsky-timeline

[93]https://www.vox.com/2018/10/15/17978156/hillary-clinton-monica-lewinsky-interview-bill-clinton-sexual-misconduct-metoo

transparently wrote about in a beautiful piece for Vanity Fair where she describes herself as a "modern day scarlet letter." She continues,

"Maintaining that her affair with Clinton was one between two consenting adults, Lewinsky writes that it was the public humiliation she suffered in the wake of the scandal that permanently altered the direction of her life: "Sure, my boss took advantage of me, but I will always remain firm on this point: it was a consensual relationship. Any 'abuse' came in the aftermath, when I was made a scapegoat in order to protect his powerful position. . . . The Clinton administration, the special prosecutor's minions, the political operatives on both sides of the aisle, and the media were able to brand me. And that brand stuck, in part because it was imbued with power." [94]

The incessant double standard that I have been highlighting throughout this book finds its greatest example in Hillary being "disgusted" by Trump's improprieties, while she just recently went on national television to defend Bill Clinton's shenanigans.[95]

And, therefore, it appears that politics will probably *never* be the same. As a result, our beloved Washington, Jefferson, and Lincoln are no longer held on a high pedestal. Presidents are now seen as human, not some halfway divine entity, governing over us like a "guardian angel."

---

[94] https://www.vanityfair.com/news/2014/05/monica-lewinsky-speaks
[95]https://www.usatoday.com/story/news/politics/onpolitics/2018/10/15/hillary-clinton-lewinsky-affair-not-abuse-power/1649942002/

They are real people. They lie, and curse, and many are unfaithful to their wives. Do we like it? Not really. I know I don't. I want to admire, revere, and respect whoever holds the highest office in the land. A President indeed postures the climate of the nation. But I'm also a realist, and perhaps it is a fine time to recall that we are all sinners, in desperate need of a loving and graceful God. The unveiling of our Presidents as real human beings, prone to mistakes and moral failures, have given the American people the opportunity to forgive and look past their mistakes. Historically, the American populous is extremely gracious; if you admit you are wrong, ask for forgiveness, they usually grant it to you. This has also paved the way for people such as Trump, and others, to consider getting into the political arena because *most* Americans are far from perfect and have plenty they are not proud of; should this immediately disqualify them from holding office? Perhaps a century or two ago, yes. But we are in a new era and *everything* is unorthodox.

VIII. My Story

"Criticism is something we can avoid easily by saying nothing, doing nothing, and being nothing.

-Aristotle

I was sitting in the lobby at our hotel in Durham, North Carolina, waiting to check in. My oldest daughter and I had flown out from California to look at some East Coast schools for her, particularly Duke, Liberty, George Mason and Georgetown. Upon arrival, I picked up my complimentary copy of the *New York Times* and away we went to our room to relax. The horrific and saddening Parkland, FL mass school shooting had occurred the week prior so there were a few headlines still lingering, but one caught my eye immediately: "George Clooney and his wife Amal are personally donating $500,000 for the National School Walkout March Against Gun Violence."[96] My first thought was to be skeptical of anything George Clooney is personally funding, as he is a prototypical Hollywood elite who notoriously advances Left wing causes. My second was, "and what is this National School Walkout?"

[96] https://www.nytimes.com/2018/02/20/us/george-clooney-protest.html

https://rocklinhsflash.net/4790/news/localnews/the-walkout

As I read further I thought this must be some kind of joke. Schools are going to let students get up and walk out of class in the middle of the day to protest gun laws? No way. But the story seemed halfway legitimate, so I was officially put on notice that this walkout was going to take place. And then a few days later I saw that the mayor of Baltimore was going to use $100,000 of city funds to bus students to Washington, D.C. to encourage them to participate in the "March For Our Lives Gun Protest", as it was now being called. She also lured them by promising a "free t-shirt and lunch." [97] You have got to be kidding, I murmured to myself. I really didn't give it much more thought, though, after touring some beautiful colleges with my daughter and heading back to the glorious Golden State. I had *no idea* what awaited me in the next few weeks.

On Wednesday, March 7th I received an email about a staff meeting that was going to take place that afternoon with the agenda attached. I wasn't feeling good at all that day and wanted to go home and rest. So, I looked on the meeting agenda to see what I would be missing, and what to my great surprise was the #1 item:

Announcements

- March 14th National School Walkout Day- 17 minutes Amphitheater

---

[97] https://www.washingtonexaminer.com/baltimore-mayor-promises-taxpayer-money-to-high-school-students

- Optional- teacher stay back if students still in class

- Student Lead- 1st Amendment

- Teacher professionalism expected- remain neutral

- Maintain Safe School environment

A few things to note here. First, that this was an "announcement;" a "top down" decision by the administration without any discussion or input from the teaching staff. One might consider asking those who are actually *in the classroom* with students how this might affect their lesson plan, or if there are any other concerns about students getting up at 10 am and walking out for 17 minutes to protest. Second, the term "optional." This is clearly meant to imply that a teacher has the *choice* to participate or not. Why would a teacher participate in a gun protest during their contract hours? Completely inappropriate, right? The third is "Student led, 1st Amendment" gives the impression that somehow students were orchestrating this entire walkout and it was their constitutional right to do so. Arguably most people know what the 1st Amendment stipulates, but a math or biology teacher who has been long removed from their undergraduate civics course may not be too sharp on the details. (Just as I, an American History teacher, might need a refresher on the Pythagorean theorem if it was being discussed at a staff meeting.)

The next bullet point "Teacher professionalism expected- remain neutral" I almost had to laugh at; how would one "remain neutral" if they *chose* to walk out with the students? That doesn't make any sense. And the final point, of course, "Maintain Safe School Environment." I'm not sure there's anything more unsafe than randomly allowing half of the student body to walk out of class during the middle of the school day? This was foolish and very unwise, in my estimation, and I made sure the administration knew how I felt. I sent an email that explained,

"I am not feeling well at all today, so I will not be in attendance at the staff meeting, and I feel even worse now that I looked at the agenda. I am appalled that our school and staff would support ANY political protest during the scheduled day. Have we not been down this road before? There is no way that you would ever support students leaving class if they protested a conservative idea, such as abortion."

The portrayal of what the walkout was *really* about was incredibly deceptive, I thought. How dare they perpetuate a lie to an unsuspecting staff and students that this was a "remembrance" for the Parkland victims. This was a gun protest and our administration knew it. And if they didn't, then they were terribly foolish to condone a walkout when a simple google search of the event's website explicitly states that it was about protesting guns and that politics were *unequivocally* involved.[98] Compliant or uninformed, I'm not sure which one is worse?

There were so many ways that this "walkout" could have been handled, and so many examples of how it was done right. Thoughtful and objective administrators across the nation either flatly prohibited students from walking out or did what our rival school in the next town over did: A mere nine miles away from our campus is Granite Bay High School. My niece attends there so I have a firsthand account from her and my sister on how the protest played out on their campus. First, parents and students were front loaded and made aware that the protest was taking place. Second, students who truly wanted to remember the victims of the Parkland, FL shooting met *before* school to hold hands together and pray/have a moment of silence. Third, if a student did decide to get up out of class at 10 am, they had to have a note from their parent and needed to check out at the attendance window as if they were leaving school for any other reason. After the 17 minutes of protest, they were to check back in to school, with their note, and head back to class. Pretty simple and makes perfect sense, right? I don't think it took much intellect to figure out an agreeable and reasonable manner in which to handle the national walkout. That is, unless you have your own political agenda and *wanted* the protest to occur.

---

[8] https://www.nationalschoolwalkout.net

Back to the Rocklin High School campus: After I sent my email to our principal and I chose to "cc" the superintendent to ensure that he also knew that I was disappointed by their decision, I was still unsettled that this walkout was clearly being condoned. I thought to myself, "I have to at least make sure my students are informed." I have always strived to ask my students to be "free thinkers" and know *why* they believe the way that they do. (I have actually been "accused/labeled" by students over the years of being "liberal," which I take as a great compliment because it confirmed to me that I was never allowing my own personal bias into my classroom, and was challenging students who had both conservative and liberal opinions.) I am a fierce defender of the 1st amendment, and someone who *deeply* values varying viewpoints.

So, the next day, Thursday, March 8th, before my scheduled lesson on the ensuing conflict and ramifications of the Korean War, I told my students that our usual "mindful moment" (a daily 60 second, "take a pause" and reflect on the day's inspirational quote exercise) was going to perhaps take a bit longer than just one minute. The quote on the screen behind me (which was planned and I had put in my google slide presentation *long* before I even knew about the walkout) was so perfectly timed, I could hardly believe it when we read it together as a class: "*In any moment of decision, the best thing you can do is the right thing, the next best thing is the wrong thing, but the worst thing you can do is nothing."* And who was this quote by? None other than Teddy Roosevelt. Perfect and classic, I thought. Apathy and disengagement are two things that TR despised and two commonalities that are far too prevalent in our culture today. It confirmed to me that I was doing the right thing by informing and challenging my students.

The classroom conversation with my students went like this: "Are you aware of what is taking place next Wednesday?" Dead silence. Most of them knew nothing about it. I therefore gave them a brief overview and suggested that they "go research it some more on your own, and also have a dialogue with your parents." (I am a parent of two high school and two elementary students so I would definitely want to know if my own kids were planning to get up and walk out of class to protest any issue.) I then opened up the discussion and asked a few basic, but essential questions... "What do you guys think? Is it appropriate for this administration, or any administration throughout the country, to condone and allow one group of students to get up and walk out of class to protest this issue? Do you think they would give the same courtesy to another group of students? What if some chose a conservative cause to protest, such as abortion? Would they be allowed to do so during school time? What about global warming, immigration, or nuclear weapons? The list of worthy political causes to protest are seemingly endless, right?" You get the point, and so did my students. They're very bright and they understood that I was calling out the double standard.

One darling and insightful girl commented, "Mrs. Benzel, as we had just read MLK, Jr.'s *Letter from a Birmingham Jail* a few weeks ago, one thing that I remember us discussing is that if you decide to protest an issue that you are passionate about, then you need to be ready to face the consequences, as Dr. King did. If students are allowed to just get up and walk out of class without any punishment, then what is the point of protesting?" Brilliant point, I thought. She's a smart one. (Let me insert here so that it is clear: not once, or in any way, did I discourage my students from participating in the walkout; my singular goal was to ensure they were *thinking critically* and to challenge them to be sure they would support students who chose to walk out of class for an issue that they might not agree with. I never planned nor intended to thwart the national school walkout, as some have claimed.)

There were other students who chimed in and asked, "Why does it have to be a political protest? If it's truly to honor the Parkland, FL victims, then why can't we do something during lunchtime so the whole school can rally and unite together?" Excellent question, I thought. And this very insightful student gathered a few other students and made an appointment, on their own volition, with the principal. They asked him the same question... "we don't want to protest guns, but we would like to show respect to the victims. Can we float 17 balloons in the air during lunchtime with a moment of silence?" No, was the answer they were given. Why? No reason or explanation. A sufficient justification was not provided because this administration knew it was a gun protest and they clearly condoned it. The weekend , March 10th and 11th, came and went, and so did Monday and Tuesday, March 12th and 13th, of which I was on campus just as any other day. I did not receive a phone call, a visit to my classroom by our principal, nor was I asked to come to any meetings whatsoever by the administration. And then the story *really* begins:

- I was called at 8:30am on Wednesday March 14th, 2018 by our school principal informing me that I was "placed on administrative leave. Do not come in today." No reason was given. I arrive on campus at 9 am everyday so this was clearly intended to ensure I stayed home on the day of the walkout. Not exactly sure what he thought I was planning to do? Disrupt the walkout? I am not intimidating in size or stature, and I'm a reasonably amiable and well-liked teacher, so I'm not sure how much of a threat I posed but obviously enough to put me on a "time out?" What my principal did not know, and my husband can attest to, is that I stayed up until 11:30pm the night before to rework my scheduled lesson plan to minimize any distractions because I knew some students were going to get up in the middle of class. But my principal clearly did not trust me as a professional, even though I've worked with him for 20 years. (He started out as a teacher in our Social Science department and climbed his way through the ranks up to Principal. Remember the suggestion by a teacher in Chapter 1 that we "all show Michael Moore's *Bowling for*

Columbine to our students?" Yes, that was him. And here I was again...questioning and challenging him, but now he had the "power" to punish me.) I'm not sure what he thought I was going to do on March 14th with the gun protest walkout, but presumption is a very risky gamble.

- After trying to process what just happened, I called the principal back 10 minutes later and asked why I was placed on leave. Answer: "You will receive an email from the district office soon." Trying to keep things as normal as possible, I drove our two-year old to preschool at 9 am. It was drizzly and cold outside, with dark clouds looming, and I recall being so confused as to what was happening as I prayed: "I have *no* idea what is going on, but <u>You</u> do. What appears to be something horrific can only turn out to be good by Your sovereign hand." A groundswell of peace suddenly flooded my soul.

- When I got back home, I called the District Office <u>three</u> times asking for a reason. I finally received a generic letter three hours later (11:30am) that did not give any stipulations as to *why* I was placed on leave. The most alarming aspect of this generic letter stated that, "I was strictly prohibited from walking onto any RUSD property." That statement alone made me feel like a pedophile and criminal; which is exactly what most people default to when they hear that a teacher was placed on administrative leave. Teachers are not taken out of their classrooms unless they are deemed a "threat" to their students. I have children at both the elementary and high school levels; was I not allowed to go onto school grounds to pick them up? When I received this letter, I followed up with emails asking for specifics so that I could properly respond before the meeting the next day, which I was told was going to take place and I must attend, but I did not receive a reply back.

- At 3pm on this same day, Wednesday March 14th, 2018, there came a knock on our door. We are a very friendly family so our 11-year old daughter flung the door wide open and said, "Hi!" It was a darling reporter from CBS Channel 13 news. She asked, "Are you Mrs. Benzel?" To which I replied with a very confused, "yes." She then said that she had received a "tip" from a viewer that I was placed on leave. She asked if she could come inside and talk for a moment. As we started to engage, I told her that I had not been told by my district as to why I was placed on leave and she said, "Well I have the media report right here." She then read me the statement given by the outreach consultant that said, "The teacher was not placed on leave based on her viewpoints, but rather from parent and student complaints on how she conducted a classroom discussion regarding the school remembrance activities." I was *aghast* that this information was provided to a news organization without ever informing me first. She asked if I would do an on camera interview. I agreed at that moment to do so.

- At 10 pm this same night, March 14th, 2018, I received an email from my principal saying, "Because the meeting tomorrow could lead to disciplinary action, you might want to have your union representative with you." This comment was clearly intended to intimidate me, and contradicts what took place in the meeting in the bullet points below.

- I then emailed the Rocklin Teacher's Professional Association Union president at 10 pm that night...she had <u>no idea </u>any of this had taken place. The teacher's union is supposed to be notified *prior* to placing a teacher on administrative leave and the teacher is supposed to be notified, in written format, followed by a meeting, prior to being placed on leave:

ARTICLE XX PROGRESSIVE DISCIPLINE 1. This Article shall not limit the District's right to evaluate or to reprimand orally or to counsel employees. 2. (a) Normally, an employee whose work or conduct is of such nature as to possibly incur discipline <u>shall first be counseled by an administrator.</u> The administrator shall then give <u>no less than ten (10) working days to permit the employee to correct the deficiency without incurring disciplinary action</u>. Normally, at <u>least one (1) written warning shall be given before disciplinary action is imposed.</u> The employee may submit a response or rebuttal to the written reprimand or warning which will be retained in the records along with the reprimand. (b) All written warnings and employee responses, if any, shall be filed separately from the employees personnel file. In the event the Superintendent or his/her designee subsequently gives written notice to the employee of the District's intent to suspend the employee and the employee appeals, all such written warnings are admissible. 3. The District may suspend employees with or without pay for a maximum of fifteen (15) working days, pursuant to the following provisions: (a) <u>The suspension shall be based upon just cause</u>, including but not limited to: 1) Failure to follow reasonable administrative rule or directive that falls within the job description. 2) Any cause set forth in Section 44932 of the California Education XX - 2 4) A statement of the suspension proposed, including beginning and ending date(s); 5) <u>A statement that the employee has a right to discuss informally the proposed suspension with the Superintendent or his/her designee **prior** to the suspension and a proposed date, time and place for such pre-suspension discussion</u>; 6) A statement that the employee may appeal the proposed suspension by filing a grievance directly with the Superintendent or his/her designee within five (5) working days from the date of the notice of suspension; 7) A<u> statement that the employee shall have five (5) working days in which to respond to the notice of suspension</u>. If the employee does not respond, the District will schedule the suspension and provide notice thereof to the employee. The pre-suspension discussion, unless waived, shall take place within seven (7) working days from the date of the notice. (c) The pre-suspension discussion shall be informal. <u>The employee shall be given the opportunity to present facts and arguments regarding the proposed suspension.</u> (d) The Superintendent or his/her designee shall inform the employee of the decision to suspend or not to suspend within three (3) working days from the date of the pre-suspension discussion or after five (5) days from the date of the notice of suspension if the employee did not respond. In **emergency situations** requiring immediate suspension, the District may suspend with pay the employee without scheduling a pre-suspension discussion. In such emergency situations, the Superintendent or his/her designee shall schedule an informal discussion with the employee and provide the employee with written notice thereof as soon as possible after the suspension has commenced. 1) Nothing in this Article shall limit the District's right to institute dismissal and immediate suspension and mandatory leave of absence proceedings as set forth in the California Education Code, nor shall XX - 3 disciplines under this Article be regarded as a pre-condition to any proceedings under the California Education Code. 2) Suspensions pursuant to this Article shall not reduce or deprive the employee of seniority or health benefits. 3) The employee may request the presence of an Association representative at any meeting scheduled by an administrator where disciplinary action is contemplated. (underline and bold emphasis mine.)

Article XV in the teacher's contract specifically stipulates that, "the interests of <u>students are served through an open exchange of ideas and positions which include popular and unpopular views.</u> Bargaining members may include <u>controversial issues</u> and material as provided by courses of study and within the scope of the law. (underline emphasis mine.)

- At the meeting on Thursday, March 15th at 4:30pm, the first question my attorney asked was, "Is this a disciplinary issue?" To which our principal immediately quipped, "Nope, we just have some questions we want answered." This contradicts his email sent the night prior (see above). The district lawyer chimed in, "We just want this issue swept up and to get you back in the classroom tomorrow." The 6th amendment to the US Constitution specifically stipulates that "the due process of the law requires that someone is presumed innocent until found guilty." This was violated in *every* possible way. You do not presume someone is guilty, place them on leave, and *then* conduct an investigation. No probable cause was ever given.

- The next question from my attorney was, "Why was she placed on leave?" To which our principal said, "due to several student and parent complaints." He then presented us with two written student statements and one copy of a parent email. (notice the term "several." Two students and one parent does not qualify as "several.") "That's it? Two students and one parent complained and you've defamed my client's unscathed 20-year teaching record and reputation in this community?" my attorney asked. No response was given by our principal.

- They then proceeded to show us two written statements from students and one parent email. One of the student-written statements was literally 4 lines long, which caught my attention immediately. I thought to myself, "If a student is going to complain about a teacher's classroom discussion, and were given a page with which to do so, wouldn't they go on a rant and write more than 4 lines?" Hmmm. Then the parent email was given to us. Because this was unraveling in real time, we did not notice that the date and time of this one parent complaint was Thursday, March 15th at 8:42 am, constituting a full 24 hours *after* I was placed on leave. We did not even think to question whether this "evidence" was real or not because this was serious business we were conducting with high profile attorneys in the room. (More on the fictitious nature of these documents later).

- At the conclusion of the meeting, I was told that I was, "no longer on administrative leave and that they wanted me back in the classroom tomorrow, Friday March 16th, 2018." (The story had gone viral/nationwide by this point, which is precisely why they wanted this "swept up." The entire Rocklin community, past and present students and parents, as well as phone calls, emails and letters from the entire nation poured in relentlessly. I am convinced this is the *only* reason why the district recoiled immediately.)

- My union representative and the President of RTPA also told me that, "they know you are not part of the union." (As teachers, we *have* to pay union dues but I have opted out of their Political Action Committee which therefore does not give me any legal protection), and it appears that this administration presumed that I would not have anyone to represent me. Opting out of the CTA was another small but highly significant "stand." My husband, myself and one other teacher are the only three on our RHS campus who are not members of the teacher's union. This was always puzzling to me, because we chose to opt out the first year I was a teacher, prior to being tenured. But this, in my estimation, is a glaring example of the herd mentality in our culture today; no one questions anything. The CTA's PAC is extremely Left wing; I estimate that 80% of the teachers on our campus would not agree with their liberal policies but they either don't opt out or they have no idea where their union dues are going. Scary that they are possibly being led into supporting causes with their own money that they personally oppose. Ok, back to my story.

- I took the day off on Friday, March 16th, 2018 due to incredible duress suffered by not only me, but my *entire family*. My husband is also a teacher on the RHS campus, and has also served faithfully for 25 years. He is the head football coach, and is therefore much more well known in the community than I am; his obvious connection to me made people call into question his involvement and he was tethered to the situation, whether he wanted to be or not. We had two daughters at the high school level, one in 11th grade and one in 9th grade. They had to endure and try to defend numerous accusations and rumors on my behalf. We also had two daughters at the Elementary school, one in 6th grade and one in 4th grade, who had to respond to questions and provide answers regarding the situation with which they should never have had to be a part; incredible and unnecessary stress heaped on every member of our family, excluding our two-year old.

- I resumed my teaching duties on Monday, March 19th, 2018. *Everything* on campus was different; the atmosphere, tone, and heavy weight that I felt; my reputation was ruined. I felt completely undermined as an instructor and that I had lost my students and co-staff's respect. Speculation ran rampant everywhere.

- One of the parents of the students whose written complaint was provided as evidence sent me an email me on Tuesday, March 20th and requested a meeting. I asked if this parent wanted the administration to attend and this parent said no. We met in the small conference room on campus. This parent preceded to tell me that, "our students did not go down to the office voluntarily to complain about your conversation in class, but were rather called out of class by the female vice principal. They were called down separately, no one else was in the room, like a parent or other adult should have been, and they were asked leading questions to attain the narrative that they desired. Our students were used as pawns to target you. I know these things first hand because I conduct interviews for a living. Our students were really upset when they heard you were placed on leave and how this harmed you, and said they were confused and felt used." "Wait, *what*?!?," was my response. This is, by far, the most crucial component of this entire situation. My students, who I adore earnestly, were *used* to get information to harm me? This was a game changer.

- As soon as I left the meeting, I went straight to my classroom and immediately sent an email to all parties involved letting them know what had just transpired: the District Superintendent, both attorneys, the principal and female vice principal, and my union representative. I shared with them the contents of what this parent had told me. *Nothing* was acknowledged or done in response. <u>Nothing</u>. And nothing has been said or done since. I have never been called into a follow-up meeting to discuss any of the events that have taken place. It has remained extremely unclear what the District's intention was on this is, but when I inquired with my union President as to the status of my situation, she suggested, "I think they are just hoping it will go away." Incredulous, I thought.

- Without question, I *was* targeted. This administration went on a "hunting expedition" to get supposed evidence to use against me. The talking points as to why I was placed on leave from the district office have changed **three times**, all the while none of this has *ever* been stated to me in verbal or written format. Perhaps the bottom line is that my principal couldn't handle me challenging his decision to condone the gun protest walkout and told me to stay home so I wouldn't be disruptive?

- And, by the way...the media report given by the school district that the school walkout was condoned because it was a "school related remembrance activity" is misleading in every possible way. Our school newspaper, The Flash, covered the event with the following headline, "Rocklin High School students banded together to host a walkout in protest of the lack of action in gun reform. The event took place in the outdoor amphitheater at 10 am, following the guidelines of the #NationalSchoolWalkout." One student, who participated, clearly demonstrates my point: "I'm here to support anti-gun laws. Partly for the lives, but this is mainly political."[99]

---

[99]https://rocklinhsflash.net/4790/news/localnews/the-walkout

Students on the Rocklin High School Campus Protesting Gun Laws 14 March 2018

Flabbergasted yet? As I alluded to in Chapter 1, taking a stand can be lonely and extremely isolating. When I was placed on leave, very few colleagues in my teaching community reached out to me; I was both disheartened and disappointed by this. If I had heard of a teacher placed on leave that I knew or had interacted within the community, at the very minimum I would have sent them an email asking, "Are you ok?" It would not matter what I had heard or thought of the situation, I would extend the benefit of the doubt and seek clarity from them, not the "chitter chatter" elsewhere.

Taking a stand may not be popular, and it's usually not, but incidents like this show the true nature of people, don't they? It confirmed for me why Jesus chose only 12 disciples and not 25. Our small world that I've trusted as personal confidantes has grown even smaller as a result of my situation, but that's ok. Pruning the vine of unnecessary influences and voices is key to taking a stand: Be firm in your convictions, graceful in your approach, and steadfast to the end. One bright gem in all of this, however, was the resource aide teacher who was in my classroom the day I had the brief dialogue with my students about the gun protest walkout. On her own volition, she offered the following: "If you ever need a witness to testify to what you said or how you conducted your classroom that day, I will gladly come to your defense. You didn't do or say anything wrong." It sure would have been nice if the administration would have consulted this well-respected and longtime aide about my discussion that day, rather than pulling two of my students out of their class, separately, and forcing them to manufacture evidence to use against me. Or, here's a wild thought…ask *me* what I said in class?

To close out my situation, three months had passed since I was placed on leave, it was now June, and the school year was winding down. I had, in the meantime, put my nose back to the grind, working tirelessly for my students, loving on my family, attending ball games on Saturdays and serving at church on Sundays. And then the thought occurred to me…*nothing* has been done since this fiasco broke; no follow-up meeting, email, or phone call. I have never been told what I did wrong and no one has been held accountable in *any way*. Not one attempt to acknowledge or rectify this situation at all. There was no way I could return to a campus and work for an administration that is obstinate, arrogant and that I do not respect - especially when one of the teachers on my campus informed me that our principal had declared just days before in a department chair meeting regarding my situation, "I am not giving in and I am not apologizing." Wow, I thought. The power of a personal or public apology would have changed the entire course of these events, but pride is a powerful thing indeed.

Upon these revelations, I took my final and ultimate stand. I filed a grievance for the sole purpose of protecting ALL teachers on my campus from ever having to incur harassment like this again. However, the district office rejected my grievance because it was not filed "in time." Apparently, there is an 8-day window when one must gather all this crucial and necessary evidence, as if there would ever be a possibility to do so under such extreme time constraints. My grievance stipulated three *very specific* violations of my contract on the part of this administration. The powers that be will have their way for now, but that is why it is crucial that my story be told in its entirety.

Has my life changed? Drastically. If you knew our family before this incident, you would realize that we are the most ordinary, average, and private people of all. My husband and I adore our five daughters and have invested every minute of our time, (outside of our school and church) into their development. We don't seek fame or fortune; we are high school teachers so clearly money has never mattered to us. We didn't have social media because nothing we did was exceptional or exciting enough to post. So that brings me to my next point: My decision to run for President of the United States.

Am I insane? Have I lost it? Perhaps. The small circle of trusted mentors in my life, (my husband being the first and foremost) don't think so, nor does my pastor's wife who is the second most important barometer in my life. But we understand how and why many people do. Yet, as I reflect through the annals of America's most influential people, it is those who are *crazy* enough to think that they can change the world, are the ones who actually do. Who do I think I am to file with the FEC to run for POTUS?

Well, give me a moment here and I'll explain. When the initial story from our local CBS Channel 13 news broke, it went viral the next day: Ben Shapiro's Daily Wire, the Washington Examiner, New York Post, Dennis Prager, Larry Elder, the Blaze, David Knight, Armstrong & Getty, and a myriad of other national and local radio and online shows picked it up and called me for interviews. But perhaps it was Fox News Channel that turned the tide. (I kept waiting for Chris Matthews, Jake Tapper or Rachel Maddow to call, but they never did.) First and foremost, this was a

1st Amendment issue, but one would have to be incredibly insightful and intelligent to understand that. Fox & Friends contacted me, then Tucker Carlson Tonight, and then the Ingraham Angle. The impact of these three iconic media outlets, coupled with the unbelievable show of support from not only my current students and parents, but those from five, ten, and fifteen years ago who wrote letters, emails, and phone calls to the school on my behalf was unexpected and overwhelming. Flowers, balloons, and gift cards awaited me at school upon my return. I felt vindicated and that perhaps my 20 years of teaching had made an impact after all.

But there was more. So much more. I was receiving at least 20 emails *a day* from people as far away as Alaska, Minnesota, Florida, and Maine. I tried my best to keep up with them, and wanted to genuinely respond to each one, but it got to the point that I simply had to click the generic option, "thank you so much" as a reply. Voicemail messages from Virginia, Arizona, Ohio and Texas poured in. (One US Marine veteran asked me to call him back, so I did: his voice quivering on the other end, "I risked my life and served this country for you to be able to ask the kind of question that you did. Thank You. I hope to call you Madame President one day.") Really, I thought? Where is this coming from? I'm not the hero in all of this... that original local reporter is the one who had the brazen courage to come find me and knock on my door at 3pm in the afternoon. Were it not for her boldness, I have no doubt that my school was going to punish me somehow. I don't know how (or why) but they were surely after me.

And then when I finally got around to my teacher's box in the front office the next week, I was aghast: handwritten letters piled up. What is this, I thought? Letters...who writes letters anymore? They poured in from all corners of the country: Nevada, Oklahoma, North Carolina, Rhode Island, and Maine. Keep in mind that I was not on any social media whatsoever so these people were taking their own valuable time to go to the Rocklin High School website and find the information that they needed to send an email, leave a voice message or write a letter. Stunning. And relentless.

My original story probably would have died down and the hype gone away, (as I suspected it would at some point) were it not for one of my very brave students, Brandon Gillespie, who pondered my original question: "Do you think this administration would support, facilitate and condone another group of students to walkout for a conservative cause, such as abortion?" He genuinely wanted to find out and test it. On his complete own volition, Brandon set up a meeting with our high school principal and had his parents and a few other students in attendance. They asked the looming question, "will you support a pro-life walkout one month from now, April 11th at 10 am for 17 minutes?" Original answer given by our principal: "I'll get back to you."

Three weeks passed and still no answer. Meanwhile, Brandon decided that he was going to proceed with this walkout whether it was approved or not. He took to social media and started a national conversation that amassed over 200,000 students across the country. He created a prolifewalkout.org website and a hashtag #life. The online interest and attention it generated was exciting, to say the least. But, of course, not everyone shared in his enthusiasm. One week prior to the event, and after stalling with repeated requests as to whether they would support the walkout, the principal said he would not because, he said, "abortion is a controversial issue." You have got to be kidding me, I thought, when Brandon told me the next day at school. And gun control isn't controversial? And by the way, who are *you* to decide?

I'm proud to say that the Pro Life Walkout occurred. No mass funding came in, (George and Amal Clooney were nowhere to be found), no mass media coverage (USA Today did not live stream video cover this for the entire day as they did for the gun protest[100]...why not?), only the brave and tenacious Laura Ingraham highlighted it on her show that night. Our local Sacramento Bee called me for some questions but their typical

[100] https://www.usatoday.com/story/news/2018/03/13/live-stream-march-our-lives-nationwide-student-walkout-coast-coast/422723002/

liberal coverage was so slanted; I was so disappointed in how they portrayed the event that I will never grant them an interview again. And, by the way, the Pro Life Walkout was *truly* student led, unlike the Gun Control Walkout which was gravely manipulated and fully scripted by billionaires, politicians and the mainstream media. My two daughters participated in the Pro Life Walkout, along with about 30 other courageous students. They brought the karaoke speaker and microphone that we use at home since they weren't granted the large PA system by the school. It was a bit drizzly that day but they braved the cold, dark clouds, as no tents were provided for them either. There were about 5 counter protesters with "My Body, My Choice" signs, something I highly doubt the administration would have tolerated during the gun protest walkout: another view from a different group of students. The event was a bit unorganized because, let me reinforce this again: it was *student led*. They did not have the support of the entire nation behind them or the mainstream media hovering overhead with helicopters, cheering them on; and they were not asked to be on the cover of *Time* magazine. But they did it anyway. A very bold "stand" by these students that was inspirational, to say the least.

Do I support protesting during school instructional time? No. I never have. That was my original gripe with the National School Walkout. Classroom minutes are important and there is ample time outside of the school day (or at break and lunch) to protest in lieu of disrupting a lesson; teachers work too hard to have to manage personal politics. But, since the gun control walkout was allowed, I was in full support of these bold and unabashed students calling out the double standard.

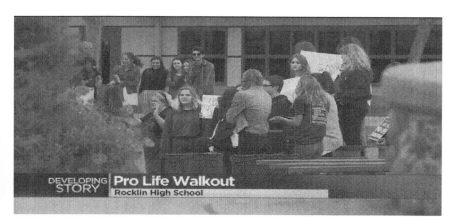

Pro Life Walkout Rocklin High School campus 11 April 2018

I was asked to do an interview on the Ingraham Angle on Tuesday, April 10 the night before the Pro Life Walkout. The result was stunning, to say the least. Laura opened her monologue stating that I had the "gall to ask if schools would support a Pro-Life walkout in the same manner they did the gun protest walkout." And then as she introduced me, she insisted, "you're a hero in my estimation." When Laura Ingraham calls you a hero, *it changes your life*. The second wave of groundswell support came in at full force and another round of emails, phone calls, and letters poured in.

"Will you please get into the national political fray?" "Can you please use your voice on a national level?" "Thank you for standing up for so many people." "Will you consider running for national office?" "We need a conservative female on the national ticket." Relentless. My husband and I had several conversations over the next few weeks. What do we do with this enormous amount of support we have received? Walk away and just go back to our sweet, lovely lives? That sure sounds nice right about now, we both thought. Recall that this was *never* in our plans. In fact, just the opposite: this past January 2018 my husband and I plotted out what we thought would be our future - teach & coach for 15 more years to get our last daughter through high school and then retire and "ride off into the sunset together." Sounds grand, doesn't it? But the weight of responsibility would not leave us. My husband suggested, "This didn't happen just so you could prove to the nation that there is a double standard. Everyone already knows that it exists. There must be something more to why this occurred." And in the lyrics of Thomas Rhett's #1 hit, *Life Changes*, (which is my official campaign song if he will allow it) "You never know what's going to happen...you make your plans and then you hear God laughing."

Our plans have certainly changed; my story is now told and the future is unknown. I'm ok with the unknown. I've jumped head first into local politics as the GOP has graciously reached out to me in a myriad of ways: Many people begging me to run for the school board, city council and county supervisor positions during the midterm Fall election cycle. I am honored to have been considered. And don't get me wrong...I love my city and I love my state. (Even though California has swung so far left one can hardly recognize her anymore.) My soul is for this *nation*. I have analyzed United States foreign and domestic policy for 30 years. I know what policies have and have not worked. I've traveled by car with my childhood best friend around this entire country for two and a half months, understanding the dynamics and demographics of each region. I believe I have a pulse on America's conscience.

This country is far from where it should be right now. The hostility we are witnessing is *not* who we are as a nation. When I read that Kamala Harris (a US Senator from California and a 2020 presidential hopeful for the Democrats), while appearing on the Ellen Show, was asked this question: "If you had to get into an elevator with Donald Trump, Mike Pence or Jeff Sessions, who would it be?" Her response? "Do they have to come out alive?" Wow. So disappointing, Kamala, in every way. And you want to be our President? No thank you. Do you know how I would answer that question if Ellen asked me, "If you had to get into an elevator with Hillary Clinton, Barack Obama, or Elizabeth Warren?" I would genuinely reply, "How about *all three*? I can get into an elevator with anyone and have an amiable and glorious exchange of ideas. Who knows, maybe we'd even go grab some coffee together afterward."

So, yes, I'm running for President. Am I qualified? I think perhaps. But then again, who is really "qualified?" Donald Trump's Populist victory thrust the door wide open for people like me who never even considered political office before. But I believe the Framers of the US Constitution would have approved of my candidacy; the stipulations are quite clear on who can run: Be a natural born citizen, resident for 14 years and thirty-five years of age. I meet those requirements. If the Founding Fathers welcomed and encouraged average citizens to run for high office, so why not throw my hat in? I am a sincere capitalist who highly values competition. Iron sharpens iron, and the best candidate will emerge if there are more of them. Americans deserve options.

May I suggest a few things that I have in my favor? I can immediately tap into talented and intelligent millennials, (I taught them for over 20 years and most of my students went to the premier universities in California and the East Coast), many of whom have already contacted me and are ready and eager to join my campaign. If you think JFK had the "best and the brightest" cabinet, wait until you see mine. I'm a mom with five kids. The one commonality among women is the bond of motherhood.

It doesn't matter where you're from, what you look like, what religion you practice (or don't), whether you have a college degree or not, a mother's heart is easily recognized. I can talk to *any* mom, *any* time, for *any* reason. Moms endlessly multi-task and I would genuinely love to see this nation guided by a Mom; the results, I believe, would be stunningly impressive.

Do Black Lives Matter? You bet. My Master's Thesis specifically focused on the activism of the African American church in the Civil Rights Movement. As addressed earlier in this book, we have made significant steps forward with race relations in this country but there is still plenty of progress to be gained. Every life matters. Every person who identifies as LGBTQ, and everyone who does not. Those who support gay marriage and those who support traditional marriage. And when I say every life matters, I mean *every* life.

I know what it feels like to be faced with an unplanned pregnancy. My husband and I had four beautiful daughters intentionally. We were perfectly content and in a wonderful "groove" of life. And then when I was 44 years old, we found out we were expecting another, seven years after our last daughter was born. I was stunned and shocked, and we were in the middle of football season, so I waited two months to even tell my husband. I could hardly process the news myself, how was he going to react? Not speaking for a few hours was how he responded. At my first appointment, I bawled in my doctor's office. Pretext: I had all four of our daughters by C-section, so a fifth was going to be very risky; my doctor said the placenta needed to be at "just the right place to avoid complications for both you and the baby." "Do you want to do any testing prior?" my doctor asked. "No," was my response. "We're keeping whatever comes out of me." A man of great faith, he then assured me, "God does not make mistakes." The ensuing months were wracked with a mixture of fear, hope, anxiety, and excitement. But what was the result? Another beautiful, healthy baby girl who has transformed our entire family into a dynamic we never thought possible, and we cannot *fathom* our lives without her. This has turned our oldest two daughters into the most nurturing and selfless teenagers I have ever seen. Our younger two, whom we thought would feel threatened, suddenly had a new, fun and very cute playmate, and they have been thrilled to include her. (Or at least most of the time!)

We all had to adjust, of course. This was, after all, an *inconvenient* blessing. We were starting over, in a sense, and it was not easy. Did I really want to nurse a baby at the age of 45? And wake up at 3am in the morning to do so? Not especially. And then maintain order in our household, support my husband and go teach American history? Don't forget the volleyball and softball practices and games, coupled with making lunches and who could forget homework? Exhausting, yes. But just like the rest of you, we work hard because we know it all matters in the end. Am I opposed to abortion? Unequivocally. Do I want to overturn *Roe vs. Wade*? If one truly knew the supreme court ruling (which was another example of judicial activism and legislating from the bench), then they would understand that the 7-3 majority opinion stipulated that abortion is to be "safe, legal, and *rare*." [101] If we look at the so-called feminists today, they are literally touting that they've had an abortion, virtually applauding and celebrating it like it's some kind of badge of honor.[102] Seeing Gloria Steinem wear a shirt that says "I had an abortion", shouting it to the whole world is such a disgrace. Cecile Richards', former President of Planned Parenthood, stated goal was to "destigmatize abortion in America",[103] but that simply has not happened. Although 71% of Americans still want abortion to be legal, even more (82%) suggest that it should be just as it was ruled in *Roe v. Wade*: rare. Terminating an eight-month old baby in the womb should never, ever be allowed. [104] So let's shift the conversation from "overturning *Roe v Wade*" to reinforcing *Planned Parenthood v Casey*, 1992. The Supreme Court reaffirmed the basic principles in *Roe* that a state cannot outlaw abortion altogether, but

[101] https://supreme.justia.com/cases/federal/us/410/113/
[102] https://www.dailywire.com/news/32911/when-abortion-becomes-sacrament-ben-shapiro
[103] Richards, Cecil. *Make Trouble*. New York: Simon & Schuster, 2018.
[104] http://www.pewforum.org/fact-sheet/public-opinion-on-abortion/

stipulated that it could regulate abortions at any point after fetus viability, so long as the law contains exceptions for pregnancies which endanger the woman's life or health.[105]

For example, a parent of a minor must be notified and acknowledge that they are aware prior to an abortion. Five states have "window to the womb" laws that require that the mother view an ultrasound (24-48 hours prior) to having an abortion; a majority of other states give women the option to see an ultrasound.[106] And this is where my heart is also: I would never want a woman to have to resort to a "back alley, unregulated seedy clinic" to get an abortion, but this is far more of a talking point by the Left than what would actually ever occur. There are so many alternatives to aborting a baby; my sincere desire is that it would be a woman's absolute *last resort*. The abortion debate is not about "choice," or controlling one's body, but advocating for an unborn life that should at least have a chance to survive.

So, there's my platform. Am I really that significant? I don't think so. To my small world here in Rocklin, California perhaps; to my family, most assuredly. But therein lays my overall point: I have taken small, but solid stands in my twenty years of being on a public high school campus

---

[105] https://supreme.justia.com/cases/federal/us/505/833/

[106] https://www.bbc.com/news/world-asia-china-43361276

and it has all come to a pivotal point. Assessed individually, they may seem irrelevant and meaningless, but the totality of speaking truth to power counted for something on March 14, 2018. My stand was revealed, the nation vehemently came to my defense, and it changed the way I thought about almost everything: Perhaps my husband and I weren't put on this earth to "bleed Rocklin High blue and silver" after all, we thought. Pouring our blood, sweat, and tears into our school and community for two decades didn't seem to count for much after all. But, perhaps, it will mean something someday. That will be up to you to determine. What we have decided as a family is that we can no longer sit back and let this incredible country of ours be torn apart; we commit to being part of the solution. "United Forward" is our campaign slogan, and we march with it into 2020.

IX. In Search of the Ordinary

"Progress in America does not usually begin at the top and among the few, but from the bottom and among the many. It comes when the whispered hopes of those outside the mainstream rise in volume to reach the ears and hearts and minds of the powerful."

-Jon Meacham, The Soul of America: The Search for our Better Angels

I am not alone in my stand. There are many others out there: Every day, average Americans who are strong in their convictions and unwavering in their faith. And we need more people who are willing to rise and be heard for what they believe in, even if in the seemingly smallest of ways. One of the biggest lessons I learned from my recent incident is that marginalized voices may not always be the loudest, but they certainly are voluminous- as was attested to by the incredible and unexpected response to me being placed on administrative leave by people from all over the country.

Why was the groundswell of support for me so intense? I think it resonated with a great majority of Americans that it was absolutely absurd that I was punished for asking my students to think critically and for simply calling out the double standard. And it wasn't just conservatives. I have held on to an email from a woman that I will probably never meet, but she wrote to me and said,

> "I will happily contribute money and I am sure thousands and thousands would as well to you and any campaign you embark on. You tried to inject thought-provoking questions, something good teachers do, and you were slapped down for it. They set the tone and sent a message through your suspension which was play by their rules or suffer consequences. As a side note, I would also give additional monies to a religious student group that wanted to stage a pro-life walkout to support your point even though I am a liberal, pro-choice woman. This is exactly the kind of thing that has been happening on college campuses for years and apparently, is finding its way into high schools now."

It's worth noting that this email was sent to me the day after my suspension, before my student, Brandon Gillespie, took up the challenge to test the double standard, so she did not know that a pro-life walkout would be occurring the next month. I will be seeking out people just like this woman to work on my staff and in my cabinet...*true patriots* who may not share my political views but who revere our Constitution and its protections for *all* Americans, not just those we agree with. This email is *still* sitting in my inbox and I will probably keep it there forever because I treasure it that much. It reminds me that there is great hope for our country because of people like her.

Fortunately, the woman who sent that email is engaged in the pertinent discussions of our time, but many are not. Do most Americans pay attention to the political clamor and noise? Probably not. And many are disinterested because of the incivility we see on our television screens each night. Who could blame them?

When I announced that I was running for President, I had more than a fair share of my close friends and former students say to me, "Well, I guess I better register to vote then." Most of them are in their thirties. Lazy, apathetic millennials? Perhaps. But I'll offer another possibility: They don't feel like much can really be done. And why should they? With a $21 trillion deficit, how does one even begin a conversation with an average American as to how to tackle this incredible crisis? As the National Priorities Project put it, "The vision of democracy is that the federal budget – and all activities of the federal government – reflects the values of a majority of Americans. Yet many people feel that the federal budget does not reflect their values and that the budgeting process is too difficult to understand, or that they can't make a difference."[107] And when I dialogue with students and parents about the enormous and overwhelming cost of college tuition, they mostly shrug their shoulders as they walk away because they think, how will it change? [106]

106 https://www.nationalpriorities.org/
107 https://www.insidehighered.com/news/2017/10/25/tuition-and-fees-still-rising-faster-aid-college-board-report

A robust and respectful national dialogue is a great place to start. As I have had the privilege to engage with some of the best minds in this country over the past 20 years, one thing I know for sure: If we ask the right questions, we can get some pretty insightful responses. Do I think I have all the answers? Not even close. If we can tap into the incredible resource that are the American people, I think we might be surprised with the results. The very first step of my campaign will be to embark on a two-month, "fact finding" bus tour. Similar in nature to Salena Zitos' trip to the Heartland to understand Trump's America,[108] my family and I will be visiting the most common venues to engage with *real* Americans to ask what concerns them most; we'll most definitely head to the Iowa State Fair. We can hardly wait.

Not just Heartland Americans, however, but Americans from every corner of this incredible nation need to be consulted and their voices need to be heard. I love it whenever I see Trump gathering people at the White House and *listening* to their voices. There is great strength and great humility in not having to speak all the time, and in asking others, "What do *you* think?"

---

[107] http://thefedederalist.com/2018/08/03/8-insights-from-salena-zitos-book-about-trumps-america

http://www.governing.com/gov-institute/voices/col-dysfunctional-general-services-administration-impact-states-communities.html

Will I be an expert on a wide range of topics? Probably not. But this I *can* tell you: What the Washington "elites" know, I can always learn; they will never understand the experiences I have had as a real, ordinary, average American. I'll tell you exactly who my first hire will be: Dana Perino. As I read her articles and listen to her commentary, I am strengthened and encouraged by her tone, demeanor, and insight on an array of issues. And, I will most definitely find a position for Greg Gutfield; he is so hilarious, I would want him around for sheer perspective and morale.

I'd love to draw Condoleezza Rice back into the political arena, and add Marie Harf to the short list also. Although Marie worked for the "other side" (oh no!), she is sharp, fair, and reasonable. Peter Bergen would be my absolute top choice as adviser to the Middle East if I can lure him out of his consulting contract with CNN. Reihan Salam, National Review editor and author of the newly released *Melting Pot or Civil War: A Son of Immigrants Makes the Case Against Open Borders,* offers some bold new ideas on how we can move past the myopic talking points on immigration, and enact lasting reforms. I'll offer him a position as well. I thoroughly admire and welcome his unorthodox approach. I want to hear as many viewpoints as possible on a given topic to make a fully informed and objective decision. (As a side note, an additional campaign pledge of mine will be: "This commandment will I keep, I shall not tweet more than once a week.") Americans have better things to do than hear from me at 3am in the morning.

The apparatus of Washington, D.C. is firmly in place and there are people whose entire lives have been spent studying the surmounting debt and working at the Congressional Budget Office trying to figure out how to tackle it. I know enough to understand that with all the chatter about Russia, North Korea, and Iran, we should be paying much closer attention to China as a looming threat in the 21st century. President Xi's term limits were just eliminated so he can remain in power for life, our trade deficit with China is growing, and their slow but steady encroachment into the South China Sea are all of pertinence to US interests at home and abroad.[109] And China is one of the rare topics that creates a consensus among politicians: Nancy Pelosi and Chuck Schumer are in alignment with President Trump and the Republican Party on their stance against this ensuing threat. My administration will tap Michael Pillsbury of the Hudson Institute who articulates the importance of this issue brilliantly in *The Hundred Year Marathon: China's Secret Strategy To Replace America as the Global Superpower*. Let's start on an issue such as China and build unanimity from there. I will harken back to the precedent set by George

---

[109] https://www.bbc.com/news/world-asia-china-43361276

Washington to have opposing views in my administration. He tapped Alexander Hamilton and Thomas Jefferson to key positions in his cabinet precisely because they held varying ideas, and he listened to both of their proposals before making his decisions; the constitutionality of the Bank of the US is the most notable. A wise one, indeed, was Washington. He was also greatly disturbed by political factions and their potential to tear the country apart:

> How unfortunate, and how much is it to be regretted.., that whilst we are encompassed on all sides with avowed enemies and insidious friends, that internal dissentions should be harrowing and tearing our vitals. The last, to me, is the most serious-the most alarming-and the most afflicting of the two. And without more charity for the opinions and acts of one another in Governmental matters. ... I believe it will be difficult, if not impracticable, to manage the Reins of Government or to keep the parts of it together: for if, instead of laying our shoulders to the machine after measures are decided on, one pulls this way and another that, before the utility of the thing is fairly tried, it must inevitably be tom asunder- And, in my opinion the fairest prospect of happiness and prosperity that ever was presented to man, will be lost-perhaps forever! [110]

I don't think it's too far of a stretch to suggest that Washington would have abhorred the political climate today. As suggested earlier, we need more and more ordinary, average Americans to rise to the call and become actively engaged in the process to make any real change possible.

I also think most of our Founding Fathers would be aghast at the behemoth

[110] https://www.dailysignal.com/2016/02/11/what-we-can-learn-from-jefferson-hamilton-debate-on-national-bank

and bloated size of the Washington Establishment elite. Trump vowed to "Drain the Swamp," which was a great start. I will personally drive a Cat D11R and "Bulldoze the Bureaucracy." We can see if/when/how long the American people notice that some buildings in DC have been leveled as a barometer of whether to rebuild them or not. Green grass and beautiful trees growing in the place of the General Services Administration[111] building might be really refreshing? Here is what the Heritage Foundation discovered about government agencies and their overlapping roles:

Consolidating duplicative programs will save money and improve government service. In addition to those programs that should be eliminated completely, Congress should consolidate the following sets of programs:

- **342** economic development programs;
- **130** programs serving the disabled;
- **130** programs serving at-risk youth;
- **90** early childhood development programs;
- **75** programs funding international education, cultural, and training exchange activities;
- **72** federal programs dedicated to assuring safe water;
- **50** homeless assistance programs;
- **45** federal agencies conducting federal criminal investigations;

---

[111] https://www.gsa.gov/

- **40** separate employment and training programs;

- **28** rural development programs;

- **27** teen pregnancy programs;

- **26** small, extraneous K-12 school grant programs;

- **23** agencies providing aid to the former Soviet republics;

- **19** programs fighting substance abuse;

- **17** rural water and waste-water programs in eight agencies;

- **17** trade agencies monitoring 400 international trade agreements;

- **12** food safety agencies;

- **11** principal statistics agencies; and

- **Four** overlapping land management agencies.[112]

Almost mind boggling, isn't it? And now you wonder why some of my friends are not even registered to vote? How can they comprehend such reckless behavior in our government? And why should they care? Remember, these are every-day, average Americans who are busy working at their jobs, engaged with their families and communities.

As I reflect more and more on the ordinary nature of my life, and recalled yet again when Laura Ingraham said, "You're a Hero in my estimation because you had the gall to ask if a school would allow a walkout for a conservative cause," I was genuinely taken aback...did Laura

[12] https://www.heritage.org/budget-and-spending/report/top-10-examples-government-vaste

Ingraham just say that I was a *hero*? Me? There are plenty of others out there who have taken their own stands. Sean Sweet, a fifth grade teacher in Lincoln, CA tells of his encounter in a "politically correct" charged era:

"Eagle Head" Bless America

- I was a school teacher for seven years. I had established great relationships with the other staff members and with the community in which I served. It was a small rural K-8 school. When the new principal came, things changed.

- In September of 2002, she instructed each teacher to have their students create a patriotic banner of some kind to put in front of the school to commemorate the one year anniversary of 9-11. Each class was given a large sheet of butcher paper and told to send up their finished banners before lunch.

- Teaching 5th grade, I had learned that preteens are motivated to do well with something when it is their idea, so I made this a leadership/team assignment and sat down in the back of the room while the students went through the process I had taught them to brainstorm and select an idea that they could reach consensus on.

- Their idea: make the banner into a large American flag and write the words "GOD BLESS AMERICA" across it. I double checked. "Does anybody have any objections to this?" No. "Are you sure? You all like this idea?" Yes. I knew better than to try to censor their speech, so I let them get started creating their banner. Every student worked to create the banner as a group, and two of the students brought it to the office.

- When I brought my class to lunch, there they were: the banners were all hung across the front of the school. But something was different about our class' banner. The principal had covered over the word "GOD" with a picture of a giant eagle head.

- I was immediately concerned. After getting the run-around with the principal who wouldn't hear my concerns, I called the district office. I didn't want to be in the middle of an issue of this magnitude with the parents of the students

148

who had, completely of their own free will, decided to express themselves with the words "God Bless America." I left a message for the superintendent.

- In the afternoon, there was a knock at my classroom door and who should walk in? The superintendent himself. He came in to explain why the principal had done what she did. His explanation was obviously unrehearsed or well-thought through, and I'll never forget that he wrote on the classroom's whiteboard as he spoke. At the bottom of his diagram which accompanied the weak explanation, he wrote dollar signs. I took a mental picture of those dollar signs. Was this really the concern?

- I'm pretty sure before coming into our classroom, the superintendent reprimanded the principal, because after this she was not friendly toward me at all. I tried to explain to her that I was just trying to make sure that we weren't involved in any kind of lawsuit from upset parents, and she just angrily shook her head at me. She looked at me and said, "And you call yourself a Christian," as she closed the door to her office.

- For the rest of the year, she made comments and facial gestures that showed me what she thought of me being a Christian.

- Teachers were supposed to arrive 30 minutes before the bell rang each day, and within a month of the "Eagle Head Bless America" incident, I was written up (for the first time in 7 years) for being on site 28 minutes before the first bell rang. That's right. She wrote me up for being two minutes late on 1 day out of the over 1,000 days that I worked as a school teacher.

- At the end of that same year, the principal gave me a very poor review (I had never received anything but all "excellent" marks before then) and was mandated to attend teacher training in the summer in order to continue in my position. I resigned and became a youth pastor.

There are more like Sean Sweet's story. So many more. You've probably heard many stories yourself, or even been a part of one. Your

149

stand is just as important as mine. And we must continue to stand. We don't fight, but we do *battle*. We are intense warriors that will not relent in the face of threats and intimidation. We do so in a spirit of love and genuine humility. There is room for disagreement, yes. But there is never room for blatant and overt silencing of any one or any idea. This is what we must continue to stand against.

I am fortunate that I have received a tremendous amount of support from my local community: the Placer County GOP Central Committee immediately reached out to me and appointed me to be a representative for District 3. We were primarily focused on electing John Cox as our next Governor, helping Tom McClintock get reelected to the House of Representatives, repealing SB54 known as the "sanctuary state" status, passing Proposition 6 to repeal the gas tax in California, and how to effectively galvanize these into a major movement for the Fall elections. We were also raising awareness and strategizing for local school board and city council candidates, and I am speaking to a variety of groups to ensure that voter apathy does not remain the norm. "Midterms Matter" was my motto for the Fall election. Ordinary people doing extraordinary things causes significant change in the world. Let's go do it!

X. Resist? How about REVOLT

"The Tree of Liberty must be refreshed from time to time with the blood of patriots and tyrants."

-Thomas Jefferson

The vitriol that has ensued since the 2016 election has only intensified over time. It has already been discussed in previous chapters, but it is worth repeating that our nation is incredibly divided. My morning routine consists of pulling up a variety of news sources: As a historian, I try to consult an array of opinions. I seek objectivity over hyperbole. I start with DailyWire and then Vox, but the two worlds could not be more polar opposite. Rarely is there a story on both websites that even nominally resemble each other. I then pull up National Review, TownHall, and The Federalist, concurrent with Politico, Slate and the HuffPost. I listen to Dennis Prager and Tom Sullivan on the radio as much as possible. I have a subscription to *Time* magazine and I'll read USA Today from time to time.

I'm committed to consulting a wide range of sources and opinions because I do not, nor will I ever, live in a bubble. I still believe there is far more commonality among us than there are differences. After all, our DNA is 99.95% the same; surely we don't need to focus on the remaining .05% do we? And yet, the hysteria on the Left is mostly *manufactured* in my opinion. True division in this country occurred in 1861 and 1968; the Civil War and Vietnam/Civil Rights Era were divisions that led to a much greater country: The abolishment of slavery and the expansion of equal rights. Today's climate is toxic to the point of denigrating the principles we hold dear as Americans: respect toward our fellow man, civic discourse, and the ability to amiably disagree. We cannot afford to lose these.

It's been incredibly disheartening to watch the "other side" come unglued at every turn; I did not vote for Barack Obama, but I didn't lose my mind over it and commit the next four years of my life to "resisting" everything he did. I would have genuinely loved to vote for the first African American president, but unlike the Left, I do not engage in identity politics. I look at policy positions first and foremost, and then personality and posture as a secondary factor. I was not excited about Obama's election, but I did not threaten to move to Canada or protest in the streets every weekend. The pendulum shift in this country never swings one way for very long. It might behoove all Americans to revisit a History 101 course to realize that this *will not last*; if one side has better ideas and better candidates, then they ultimately win elections. It is not, in my estimation, worth tearing the country apart simply because you didn't win; get over it and work harder next time.

Perhaps there is no better example of how low we have sunk than the recent confirmation hearings of Brett Kavanaugh. The Supreme Court, our most sacred institution, has been wracked with a bipartisanship that I have never seen, heard or read about in our nation's history. Nominees have always been treated with the dignity that they deserve; the Supreme Court has remained refreshingly "above the fray." Yet, no matter where you fall on the political spectrum, you cannot argue that Kavanaugh has been treated fairly. The "spartacus" and "moral" moments of Cory Booker were almost too much to watch;[113] never has such blatant drama and showmanship entered this arena. I was seriously embarrassed for him.

In this #MeToo Era, everyone must be heard and the evidence must prevail; we cannot lose due process in this country. No one is suggesting that Dr. Christine Ford is disingenuous in her recollection of events; her testimony was certainly heartfelt and compelling. But if the allegations against Kavanaugh were known since July 2018, why were they held onto until the 11th hour, right before his confirmation vote? Six FBI investigations have already been conducted on him and not one trace of these sexual allegations was found[114]. From the outside observer, it

---

[113] https://www.heritage.org/political-process/commentary/why-another-fbi-investigation-kavanaugh-would-be-pointless

certainly appears to have the stench of a political stunt. Never has a supreme court nominee been treated this way.

The "resist" movement that emerged immediately after Trump's election has done nothing except that - derail and distract at every opportunity. Is this really a way to govern? The last time I checked, it was Congress' job to legislate for the betterment of the American people. And yet, the waste in taxpayers' money continues to pile up every day; the Mueller investigation has been going on for almost two years now at a cost to the American people of $17million. As a middle class, ordinary citizen, that figure literally makes my stomach churn. To a homeless person or a single mom on food stamps, that money could be used much more wisely; I bet they would gladly take a fraction of that to better their lives. And they could care less about Russian meddling.

Which begs the question...can anything *really* be done? Are the Washington "elite" so entrenched that there is no way out? Can everyday Americans truly foment a revolution to turn over the entire establishment? The answer is YES! A quick survey through the annals of World History provides ample evidence that this *can* be done. I am not advocating a revolution with guns blazing. A peaceful, orderly transfer of power is attainable. Let's usher in another Populist Revolt, shall we? - Similar in

---

[114] https://nypost.com/2018/09/06/how-cory-bookers-spartacus-moment-fizzled-out

nature to the one that Trump started that utterly shocked the country's "ruling class."

Where to begin? First, to get more impassioned on this subject, I suggest you take a quick look at how long your current Senator or Representative has been in their position. Case in point: Diane Feinstein, (D) Senator from California, has been in Congress for over two decades and in politics her *entire* life; isn't it time to say enough is enough? Does she really think she has any idea how the crushing taxes in California affect the electorate? Or how about this one: The average wait time for service at the Department of Motor Vehicles offices statewide jumped 46 percent this year, to 69 minutes. But would most lawmakers know or care about this issue? Of course not, because they have their own office of the CDMV, an *unlisted* branch (translation: it's not widely known and most Californians have no idea this exists unless they are astutely paying attention to every detail) where elected officials can register their cars, renew their driver's licenses or apply for the new federally-mandated Real ID card. This may appear to be a miniscule infraction that our statewide politicians get their own DMV, but it is absolutely indicative of the ensuing crisis; how can elected officials have any real pulse on the American populous when they are not required to sit in line for over an hour to be seen by a DMV clerk? The answer is: *They cannot.*

I won't even get into the healthcare crisis in this country, (I have a hybrid proposal that I cannot wait to unveil to the nation) but suffice to say that while Congressional lawmakers belabor on whether to "repeal and replace" Obamacare, their lack of urgency is magnified by the fact that their healthcare "gold package premiums" are a fraction of what the rest of us pay. Try a 2 pack EpiPen for $608...or how about my daughter's asthma inhaler at $250/each? Simply unethical.

So what should we do? Here are some genuine steps that can be considered to overthrow the bureaucracy:

No person with a total net worth greater than $1,000,000,000 (one billion dollars) can hold any elected political office in the United States, from President, to Congress, to governors, to state legislatures, to mayors, all the way down to local school boards. A citizen's council will be established to continuously and independently monitor all changes in the net worth of elected officials.

US Term Limits stands up against government malpractice. We are the voice of the American citizen. We want a government of the people, by the people, and for the people- not a ruling class who care more about deals to benefit themselves, than their constituents.

Ordinary Americans could do a better job of solving the nation's problems. Most Americans (56%) acknowledge that the problems facing the country do not have clear solutions. Even so, most (55%) also say ordinary Americans could do a better job of solving national problems than elected officials.

I already alluded to what the nature of my cabinet would look like: Young and on the "cutting edge" of intellectual thought. I am intrigued by the Economic Innovation Group, and conservative millennials such as Oren Cass and Caleb Orr. I am looking for "out of the box" and creative ideas; I hope you will trust that solutions prescribed here will be voluminous throughout my candidacy and administration. How refreshing will it be to see real Americans running this country? If you're interested, I hope you will not only support Benzel 2020, but I urge you to run as a candidate yourself - in whatever capacity that may be: Local, state or national, the more "common folk" in politics, the better. Let the revolution begin today.

Epilogue

It had been six months since I was placed on administrative leave and still *nothing* had been done by my school district to rectify the situation. I finally resigned out of sheer disgust. If you haven't been able to tell by now, it has *drastically* altered our lives. I was just like the majority of Americans: I love my spouse, our girls, my community and place of employment. I've been volunteering at church for the past twenty years and there was never a plan to stop. Our family enjoys sports intensely and reading books even more. We get away to vacation at Avila Beach or Lake Tahoe whenever we get the chance. We've tried to make a difference in this world, to whatever varying degree that may be. So then, why get into the political fray? As the late, iconic and intellectual giant, Charles Krauthammer put it: "I decided to become a writer so I could discuss politics because I thought that's the most important thing one can be involved in. In the end, all the beautiful, elegant things in life, the things that matter, depend on getting the politics rights." [115] And so there you have it, that's why I've decided to run for President. What could be a more noble and worthy pursuit?

---

[15]https://www.washingtonpost.com/wpsrv/politics/opinions/krauthammer.htm

Hillary Clinton must at least be given credit for running twice and paving the rough road for women in politics. I do not agree with her policies but I respect her fortitude. We need more female leadership in the public square; women have a lot to offer. They have shaped this great nation from its inception. Although they may not have had an official vote until 1920, their imprint has been felt in every major development from 1607- the present. (If you don't believe me, read Sara Evan's *Born for Liberty*, Gail Collins' *America's Women*, or Nancy Woloch's *Women and the American Experience*.) There are daunting and formidable challenges ahead, no doubt. But America has long endured, and she will continue to long endure. No other country in the world was born out of an idea: *liberty*. To any naysayer that suggests America is not exceptional, I say, "You are unequivocally wrong." Show me a country where freedom and individual rights have been afforded to people in a greater degree than the United States. Turgot put it best when he said, "America is the best hope of the human race."[116]

Are we a perfect union? Of course not. That's why our Founding Fathers, with great foresight, put the words *Toward* a More Perfect Union into the Constitution's Preamble; they knew it would always be a work in progress. We have tried to rectify our wrongs as a nation and in the words

---

[116]https://mises.org/library/brilliance-turgot

of Thomas Paine, "We have it in our power to begin the world over again." And over and over and over again, if need be. The albeit slow-at-times progression of ideas that has moved this country from a segregated Jim Crow South to an integrated school system and society is something to be championed. The government apologized for the egregious error of Japanese American internment during World War Two. We've tried to reconcile our sordid treatment of Native Americans. And we will continue to try; treating all people with decency and respect is where we must begin again. We must be able to have reasonable discourse at the Thanksgiving dinner table again. We can't end decades-long friendships because someone voted differently than us. There is great *commonality* in the fabric of American life. We must find it and we must harness it once again. I hope you'll join me.

Acknowledgments

My darling husband Greg, and our daughters: Paige, Marin, Brooklyn, Laney and Skylar, who have come vehemently to my defense throughout this entire process. Our daily mantra of "Be Kind, Be Humble, Be Brave and Let's Attack this Day with a Level of Enthusiasm Unknown to Mankind because We Fear *Nothing*" certainly allowed us to weather this storm. We will make a great First Family. Both Kitowski and Benzel families, whose love and support have been unwavering. My Pastor's wife, Kathy Fairrington. (I could not reach my husband when I got the call that I was placed on leave. If you know him, this is no shocker. He is notoriously difficult to get a hold of and did not see that I had called and texted him about 1,000 times in an hour.) Kathy was the next person I called and she was the first to come to my aid. No questions asked. She listened, she prayed, and she personally drove me to all of my television interviews, even when we had to leave at 3:30am for one of them. Harold & Teresa Maher and Sean Sweet, who have encouraged and applauded us every step of the way, never once questioning our sanity. Tanner DiBella and Joshua Charles, two brilliant former students who believed in this project from the very start. Deborah Kern, who edited this book three times, making it sharper and clearer than I ever possibly could.

For more information on this campaign, please visit our website:

www.juliannebenzel.com

Follow us on Facebook: **Julianne Benzel for President**

Follow us on Twitter: **@juliannebenzel**

#Benzel2020

26311142R00112

Made in the USA
San Bernardino, CA
17 February 2019